How to Live Well
Despite Capitalist Patriarchy

by Trista Hendren

ISBN: 9781095608562

Cover art by Arna Baartz

www.thegirlgod.com

Please note that
none of the information presented in this book
is meant to replace advice from a medical,
health care, legal and/or other professional.
How you choose to act on the words herein
is entirely based on your own free will.
I hope this book inspires you to act
in ways that best suit your life.

A few other Girl God books...

Original Resistance: Reclaiming Lilith, Reclaiming Ourselves

There is, perhaps, no more powerful archetype of female resistance than Lilith. As women across the globe rise up against the patriarchy, Lilith stands beside them, misogyny's original challenger. This anthology—a chorus of voices hitting chords of defiance, liberation, anger and joy—reclaims the goodness of women bold enough to hold tight to their essence. Through poetry, prose, incantation, prayer and imagery, women from all walks of life invite you to join them in the revolutionary act of claiming their place—of reclaiming themselves.

Inanna's Ascent: Reclaiming Female Power

Inanna's Ascent examines how women can rise from the underworld and reclaim their power. All contributors are extraordinary in their own right, who have been through some difficult life lessons—and are brave enough to share their stories.

Re-visioning Medusa: from Monster to Divine Wisdom

A remarkable collection of essays, poems, and art: by scholars who have researched Her, artists who have envisioned Her, women who have known Her in their personal story, and then also combinations of all those capacities. All have spoken with Her and share something of their communion in this anthology.

New Love: a reprogramming toolbox for undoing the knots

A powerful combination of emotional/spiritual techniques, art and inspiring words for women who wish to move away from patriarchal thought. This reprogramming toolbox includes a mixture of compelling thoughts and suggestions for each day, along with a "toolbox" to help you change the parts of your life you want to heal.

Hearts Aren't Made of Glass
My Journey from Princess of Nothing to Goddess of My Own Damned Life—by Trista Hendren.

Single Mothers Speak on Patriarchy
More than 45 single mothers from around the world share their struggles and triumphs via essays, poems, art and critique.

The Abuse After the Abuse: How Men Use Money to Destroy Women
Co-authored by Trista Hendren and Angela Lee.
Scheduled for 2021.

Jesus, Muhammad and the Goddess
More than 35 international contributors reflect on finding Goddess within (and without) Christianity and Islam.

The Girl God
A book for children young and old, celebrating the Divine Female by Trista Hendren. Magically illustrated by Elisabeth Slettnes with quotes from various faith traditions and feminist thinkers.

Mother Earth
A loving tribute to Mother Earth and a call to action for children, their parents and grandparents.

Tell Me Why
A feminist twist of the creation story told with love from a mother to her son, in hopes of crafting a different world for them both.

See a complete list at: thegirlgod.com

Dedicated to the Memory of Cheryl Braganza

"Create in any way you can. Don't be afraid to live.
Don't be afraid to love or to be loved.
Don't just "get by."

FIGHT FOR AN EXTRAORDINARY LIFE. I did.
And you'd better do so too.
I'll be grading your performance.

See you at the top of the mountain.
I'll be waiting there for you with a bottle of Bailey's,
and a spectacular view."

-Cheryl Braganza (Feb 25, 1945 - Dec 16, 2016)

"The deed can be revoked by
re-invoking the Goddess within,
which involves 'forgetting'
to kill female divinity,
that is, our Selves."

-Mary Daly

Table of Contents

Why I wrote this book... an Introduction

Capitalist Patriarchy sucks for women.

Two years ago, I almost died. Eight weeks before that, the father of my children died suddenly—or rather not-so-suddenly for those who knew his struggles with addiction well. It was, I suppose, a long-time-in-the-making filled with pain and consequences for those who knew (and loved) him best.

I decided promptly before my emergency surgery that I *could not* die. For the sake of my children, I had to get through it—and I had to get better. I called them—fighting back tears that I vowed not to let them hear—to tell them I had to go in immediately.

My son stuttered, "Wait, *what?*"

"I will be OK," I told him—perhaps a little too harshly. "You can come see me afterwards. I love you."

It was too late in the evening for them to come by the time I was out of the recovery room. I was very happy to find myself awake however—and able to call them. I broke down and cried like a baby several times that day.

I made it through the next week in the hospital with endless YouTube healing meditations and comedies. I will never forget the kindness of the Norwegian doctors and nurses.

The doctor who broke the news to me about the tumor looked just like my beloved friend Elisabeth Slettnes, who illustrated the first three Girl God books. "Don't worry," she comforted me—as if she were my dear sister and not a total stranger. "We will take care of you just like you were one of our own."

A nurse took my hand as they were putting me under and asked how old my children were. She gave me a knowing look while stroking my arm and telling me hers were the same age. I drifted off knowing she understood exactly what was at stake.

The thought has never left me that had I been 'home' in America then, I would have been left to die—or at least bankrupt by that week in the hospital, given that they did catch it just in time. In fact, I probably would not have gone to the doctor at all. I could barely stay above water as it was. There was no option for a hefty hospital bill.

I left the United States broke, after years as a single mother. I did not have health insurance for a long time. In America, I was not even worthy of receiving child support. I was a *nothing*. Just another mother forced to figure out how to take care of her children—with little help from anyone, except my own mother.

I had done nothing to earn the kindness of these Norwegian doctors and nurses. I had not paid into their system. I was simply a human being, deserving of care on that basis alone. This is the Socialist system so many Americans are taught to be afraid of.

Angela Davis once said, "I still believe that capitalism is the most dangerous kind of future we can imagine." I finally heard her— loud and clear—laying in that hospital bed.

I had spent the prior years on auto-pilot after 6 months of family court with my ex, and then a move to Norway. Despite our ecstasy at finally being able to move abroad, it took some time for my nervous system to relax again. In my heart, I did not believe that my ex-husband would ever recover from his additions, which would enable him to have parenting time again. However, being that he came from a family with money, I also worried that we might be pulled back into some sort of family court drama again. The stress of having little say in protecting my children all those years had taken an enormous toll on me.

Before and during my 2nd marriage, I had lived in relative comfort and wealth—wanting to believe that I had somehow made it out of the confines of patriarchy. I thought I was *safe* as someone with an MBA, good income, marriage to a wealthy partner—and all the perks that come with that. But as Nawal El Saadawi reminds us, there are much larger structures at play than our individual (and sometimes privileged) lives.

> "The most dangerous shackles are the invisible ones, because they deceive people into believing they are free. This delusion is the new prison that people inhabit today, north and south, east and west... We inhabit the age of the technology of false consciousness, the technology of hiding truths behind amiable humanistic slogans that may change from one era to another... Democracy is not just freedom to criticize the government, or to hold parliamentary elections. True democracy obtains only when the people— women, men, young people, children—have the ability to change the system of industrial capitalism that has oppressed them since the earliest days of slavery: a system based on class division, patriarchy, and military might, a hierarchical system that subjugates people merely because they are born poor, or female, or dark-skinned."[1]

I used to blame myself incessantly for everything that was wrong in my life. As I grew older and began to speak more openly and honestly with other women, I began to connect the dots that make so many of us miserable. My hope is that as more women begin to wake up and share with each other, we will heal ourselves and weave our way out of this hellish maze together.

Capitalist Patriarchy thrives when women shut up and do as they are told. While it would appear (for some of us at least) that if we play by the rules, we will be safe—those of us who begin to rock

---

[1]   El Saadawi, Nawal. *Memoirs from the Women's Prison. University of California Press; Reprint edition; 1994.*

the boat with our questioning and refusal to STFU know how easy it is to be thrown off the boat altogether—children and all.

Everything within Capitalist Patriarchy is designed to keep your inner-knowing and body wisdom suppressed. Therefore, in order to thrive despite this system, you must come back into contact with the deepest parts of yourself. As females, we have been taught to deeply hate those parts of ourselves, so they are often the most hidden—buried deep within. As Monica Sjöö and Barbara Mor wrote:

> "Once we thoroughly understand how and why patriarchy acquired its power over us—the power of an entrenched mistake over the minds and lives of all people—once we understand and feel clearly that the fight of witch women is also the fight of earth's people everywhere against mechanical subjugation and exploitation—once we reestablish the magic link between the individual psyche and the earth's vital energy flow, between all-evolving matter and all-evolving spirit, and learn to encourage and teach others to do the same, in a loving return to what we always were—perhaps then, in the final time of crisis, the Serpent Goddess will shake herself loose from her deep exiled sleep in the earth's belly. Perhaps the serpent of life's flowing energy will begin to rise again, all luminous and of the earth, and the children of the Great Mother will rise up with it, and the universe will be our home again, as before. This flight is not an escape, but a return. The only way for human beings to survive the end is to return to the beginning."[2]

We must reconnect to that Serpent Goddess energy in order to regain our vitality.

---

[2] Sjöö, Monica and Mor, Barbara. *The Great Cosmic Mother: Rediscovering the Religion of the Earth*. HarperOne; 2nd edition; 1987.

A few months after my surgery, my doctor confirmed that the large tumor blocking my intestines was not cancerous. In the years since I have worked on this book on and off, at times not sure whether I should really publish it. During that period, numerous friends have discovered they had cancer or died from it. With each notification of illness or death, I was more certain that finding a way to live well under a system designed to kill us was my most important task.

I'm not a financial guru by any means—and I don't believe women are financially disadvantaged by accident. I did, however, spend 13 years as a mortgage broker and earned my MBA in my younger years, so I do know a thing or two about money. I also spent many years as a broke single mother, so I know how to stretch a dollar better than most people. Being poor requires a sort of creativity that those who are middle class and above cannot begin to imagine.

But happiness isn't all about money. You can be happy with or without it. I've lived with just about every variation there is except the very far extremes on either side. I have come to believe in the importance of naming and claiming our *own* reality—instead of passively accepting the labels and perceptions of those in power. As bell hooks wrote nearly two decades ago:

> "Women need to know that they can reject the powerful's definition of their reality—that they can do so even if they are poor, exploited, or trapped in oppressive circumstances. They need to know that the exercise of this basic personal power is an act of resistance and strength. Many poor and exploited women, especially non-white women, would have been unable to develop positive self-concepts if they had not exercised their power to reject the powerful's definition of their reality."[3]

---

[3]   hooks, bell. *Feminist Theory: From Margin to Center.* South End Press; 2000.

That said, I tried to make the most of the suggestions in this book free or as close to it as possible. If you're broke, start with free. It's always better to start somewhere than not at all.

When we examine how we are contributing to Capitalist Patriarchy with our own time, money and energy—we can reallocate our funds for things that contribute to our liberation instead of our subordination. As Arundhati Roy wrote:

> "Our strategy should be not only to confront empire, but to lay siege to it. To deprive it of oxygen. To shame it. To mock it. With our art, our music, our literature, our stubbornness, our joy, our brilliance, our sheer relentlessness—and our ability to tell our own stories. Stories that are different from the ones we're being brainwashed to believe."[4]

One of the best things that traveling and living in a different country has taught me is to question my assumptions. Many of us repeat the patterns of our families without questioning whether they serve us well. As poet Mark Gonzales asked, "Who told you the stories that taught you what it meant to be human, and did they have your best interests at heart?"

There is always a reason to worry and there is always something that you can be unhappy about. The last years have taught me to forget all that—as much as you can—and focus on what is *right* in your life and brings you joy. When you find that place in your being, it is much easier to give to others. You help no one by being a miserable person. The world has enough miserable people. Capitalist Patriarchy was designed with that very thing in mind. So, dig through all that nonsense—turn it upside down and on its head and kick it as far down the street as you can. Then, find your bliss and share it.

---

[4]   Roy, Arundhati. *War Talk*. South End Press; 2003.

While this book is dedicated to the memory of Cheryl Braganza—whose words and art inspired me immensely—it is also heavily influenced by the memory of my grandparents. My paternal grandparents, Nano and Pappa, taught me a lot about stretching the most out of life. They spent nearly 65 years together happily married. They both lived into their nineties.

My maternal grandmother, Nana, raised 5 children she had in a 6-year period—all by the age of 22. Looking at her obituary, where there is no hiding the fact that she was only 15-years-old when she married, always makes me cry. My perception is that she really did not have the life she wanted until after my grandfather died, when she confided in me that she could finally eat again.

Sadly, she died at 73—which was much too young for the healthy and vivacious woman that she was. She taught me how to stretch a food budget out in creative ways, which enabled me to feed my kids during the very lean years. She also encouraged me in her own way to leave the abusive relationship I was in with the father of my children.

All 3 grandparents taught me that you can live well no matter how little money you have in the bank. Nano used to often say that it was certain rich people who were *poor*—poor in spirit. She taught me that no matter how much you have, if you are selfish and nasty about it, you are the *opposite* of rich. As my dear friend Andrew Gurevich wrote:

> "A vitally-important and unspoken message of this failed American experiment is that even the so-called 1% do not seem to be comprised of balanced, fulfilled people most of the time. It seems that it's not just the 'losers' of this current system of unbridled, savage capitalism and its attendant institutions of repression and control that suffer all of the psychological, physical and spiritual fallout these systems produce. The elite themselves seem increasingly insecure, addicted, paranoid and discontent. Indeed, it is

7

just as George Orwell warned us so many years ago when writing about British Imperialism in the Far East, 'When the White Man turns tyrant, it is his own freedom he destroys.' The ennui hits them with an unrelenting force because it exposes the lie they have believed for generations: namely, that all they possess will make them whole. The Hindus have rightly diagnosed this psychosis by claiming a person can 'never get enough of what they don't really need.'"[5]

I started writing children's books because my own childhood was sometimes less than ideal. I wanted to do everything possible so that my children would have better lives—and that fewer children would have miserable lives. Books were my happy place—my escape route. But I realized more recently that I don't have to stay in the doom and gloom of my childhood. In fact, I owed it to myself and my children to try to have the best life I can.

This has required a lot of focus on my part. I have had to learn how to redirect my energy and beliefs. That said, I have seen how New Age thought can be toxic or dangerous to women. We simply can't will ourselves out of this existence into a commune filled with rainbows and unicorns. Genevieve Vaughan did a brilliant job of explaining the subtle, but important difference in thought.

> "It has become commonplace in the US New Age movement to talk about the co-creation of 'reality.' It is said that, by our thoughts, we cause certain things to occur and others not to occur. I hope to be able to show how we are collectively creating a patriarchal reality, which is actually bio-pathic (harmful to life), and I propose that we dismantle that reality. Our values, and the self-fulfilling interpretations of life that we make because of them, are creating a harmful illusion which leads us to act and to organize society in harmful ways. This is one sense in which

---

[5] Gurevich, Andrew. "In Goddess We Trust: America's Spiritual Crossroads." *Jesus, Muhammad and the Goddess*. A Girl God Anthology; 2016.

our thoughts do make things happen. If we understand what we are doing, however, patriarchal reality can be changed. First, we must have the courage to change the basic assumptions which serve as fail-safes to keep deep systemic changes from occurring."[6]

This book will serve as a starting point to challenge some of our societal assumptions, in hopes of helping women become stronger and breaking their chains. As we begin to heal collectively, we can overturn this system altogether.

Nothing bugs me more than someone telling me what to do—especially if they are offering unsolicited advice. Since you are reading this book, I am going to assume you want my advice—and I am going to be very candid as someone who spent the better part of four decades living in ways that did not work for me. That said, I don't really like rules myself—so if one of these suggestions doesn't sit well with you, just ignore it. It is not important to me that everyone agrees with me. My goal is that women begin to think in new and different ways from what we have been taught and socialized.

When we are separated from our sisters by secrecy, we lack the keys to unlock our cages. As Beatrix Campbell wrote:

> "Capitalism does not do life. And that lie is never more exposed in the twenty-first century than when we bring to it the light of gender and the unsaid—the silences and secrets that are knotted in the articulation of capitalism and patriarchy."[7]

---

[6] Vaughan,Genevieve. *For-giving: A Feminist Criticism of Exchange.* Plain View Press; 1997.

[7] Campbell, Beatrix. "Neoliberalism: The Need for a Gender Revolution." *Questia;* Spring 2014.

It is time to break the silences that enslave us. Just as Goddess was dethroned thousands of years ago by outright lies and defragmentation, many of the same weapons are used to weaken females today.

It is Capitalist Patriarchy's goal to keep women exhausted, ill, on-guard, ashamed, numb, distracted and defragmented so that we don't have the time or energy to battle the giant Himself. We must return to ourselves—and to Goddess consciousness—to regain our strength and overturn this abomination.

There was once another way. Let us begin to remember.

Understand What You Are Up Against

I could add several more chapters about all the hurdles females face from birth in every direction—but given how much data is readily available these days, that seems redundant.

When you take into account how many women are struggling every day just to get by—whilst dealing with PTSD and other unresolved traumas—the statistics on women and girls seem all the more bleak. The widespread use of pornography has normalized and commodified the sexual abuse of females worldwide, which could be the topic of several books. As Andrea Dworkin wrote, "When one thinks about women's ordinary lives and the lives of children, especially female children, it is very hard not to think that one is looking at atrocity—if one's eyes are open. We have to accept that we are looking at ordinary life; the hurt is not exceptional; rather it is systemic and it is real. Our culture accepts it, defends it, punishes us for resisting it. The hurt, the pushing down, the sexualized cruelty are intended; they are not accidents or mistakes."[8]

Some women literally can't tell the truth (yet). They may be in abusive relationships that are difficult to get out of safely, or fear for the lives of their children or animals. Many women are also completely dependent on a man economically (at the moment).

The topic of the widespread financial abuse of women will be the topic of an upcoming book, so I will only briefly touch on it here.[9]

---

[8] Dworkin, Andrea. "Pornography Happens to Women," copyright © 1993, 1994 by Andrea Dworkin. All rights reserved. First published in The Price We Pay: The Case Against Racist Speech, Hate Propaganda, and Pornography, Laura Lederer and Richard Delgado, eds. (New York: Hill and Wang; 1995).

[9] *The Abuse After the Abuse: How Men use Money to Destroy Women* is scheduled for later this year, and is co-written with Angela Le—sharing stories from women around the world. It has been a book that seems almost impossible to write, as the depth of the problem is endless.

As Sonia Johnson wrote, "The truth is that to displease men, to disobey them, is still deadly for women. But the truth also is that only when we stop obeying men do we truly begin to live."[10]

Many women are still brainwashed by the lies of patriarchy and can't even see their own chains.

I believe that the key to breaking free is to learn to be as honest as possible about the situation we are in. Often, this can be painful. Andrea Dworkin wrote, "Many women, I think, resist feminism because it is an agony to be fully conscious of the brutal misogyny which permeates culture, society, and all personal relationships."[11]

But what is better—living in denial or finding a solution?

Are women just supposed to have shitty lives indefinitely because men decided so thousands of years ago?

Fuck that.

I decided after my tumor-scare that I am going to have the best life I can for whatever years I have left. *I think we all should do that.* In fact, we owe it to our foremothers. They sacrificed a lot so that future generations of women could have better lives. We must begin to claim those lives.

Even if you are currently severely limited by patriarchal chains, you can still begin to gradually change your life and reclaim a little more of yourself each day. The important thing is to begin to acknowledge where you are.

---

[10] Johnson, Sonia. *Going Out of Our Minds: The Metaphysics of Liberation.* Crossing Press; 1987.
[11] Dworkin, Andrea. *Our Blood: Prophecies and Discourses on Sexual Politics.* Harper & Row; 1976.

Nawal El Saadawi wrote:

> "To live in an illusion, not to know the truth is the most dangerous of all things for a human being, woman or man, because it deprives people of their most important weapon in the struggle for freedom, emancipation and control of their lives and future. To be conscious that you are still a slave still living under oppression is the first step on the road to emancipation.
>
> We the women in Arab countries realize that we are still slaves, still oppressed, not because we belong to the East, not because we are Arab, or members of Islamic societies, but as a result of the patriarchal class system that has dominated the world since thousands of years.
>
> To rid ourselves of this system is the only way to become free. Freedom for women will never be achieved unless they unite into an organized political force powerful enough and conscious enough and dynamic enough to truly represent half of society."[12]

The time has come to take a hard look at our realities and declare new ones.

---

[12] El Saadawi, Nawal. *The Hidden Face of Eve: Women in the Arab World.* Zed Books; New Edition, 2016.

Stop Following the Damned Rules

Simone de Beauvoir wrote that, "Man enjoys the advantage of having a God endorse the code he writes... fear of God keeps women in their place." How convenient for men! Even our natural rhythms have been turned upside down and inside out—so that most of us feel like no matter what we do, it isn't good enough.

The first rule to living well under Capitalist Patriarchy is that there are no rules. In fact, you may be best served by throwing out every rule you have been taught, one-by-one.

That might sound crazy, but *who made up all these rules*—and *who benefits from them?*

As Kathleen Skott-Myhre wrote, even time itself has been manipulated.

> "Without a doubt, capitalism, as it has evolved, has fundamentally altered our sense of time. From restructuring the cyclical patterns of agricultural time into the segmented minutes and hours of industrial production, we have now moved into the indeterminate abstract temporality of virtual global capitalism. Capitalism has fully abstracted time into what Deleuze discusses as a world of infinite deferral in which one is never capable of arriving anywhere or fully achieving anything. In such a world, we are subjected to a never regime of self-improvement and training in which we are never truly adequate to the ever-shifting system of control and domination."[13]

Guess what? You can make your own rules—and create a life that works for *you*.

---

[13] Skott-Myhre, Kathleen. *Feminist Spirituality under Capitalism: Witches, Fairies, and Nomads.* Routledge; 2017.

You don't have to work around the clock taking care of everybody else or endlessly trying to improve your 'flaws.' You are already *enough,* just as you are.

If you don't believe me, try it. Break one rule at a time and make a new way for yourself.

For instance, you may think you have to get up before your family does or the world will crash. Unless you are single and your children are very small, it won't![14] I realized a few years ago that I need more sleep than my husband, but I had been in the habit of doing everything for both my kids since birth as a mostly single mom.

I had to start sleeping more after my tumor was removed, so I *did*. I slept in and everything was fine! My kids learned how to make their own lunches and find their way to school—and my husband took care of it when they needed help with something.

I'm better now, but I still sleep in longer than I used to allow myself to.

The thing is, it is human nature to be lazy and to let other people do things for you if they are 'willing' to. As women, we are socialized from birth to give TOO MUCH of ourselves to EVERYONE. And so, we end up doing EVERYTHING—and become sick, tired, frazzled and resentful.

Just *stop*.

There are very few things in this world that will collapse if you don't attend to them personally. If you can't stop for a day, or a week or a month—just try to spend 5 minutes each morning to take a moment for yourself and think.

---

[14] Suggestions on this in the *Single Mothers Speak on Patriarchy* anthology.

What do I need to accomplish today?
What is MY mission in this world?
What is MY passion?
Who am I?

Women must begin to realize how much has been stolen from us by patriarchy. We have every right to reclaim all of it. No one is going to suddenly hand it back to us, individually or collectively. We must begin to take back portions for ourselves—little by little —until *all* of it is reclaimed. Every time a woman does so, she inspires more females to do so... eventually creating a tsunami of change.

And, remember something else... If you have a daughter, she is watching you—and so are your sons. That alone is enough to make some of us stop and think. I know it did for me. Whatever toxic patriarchal patterns you manage to break, you will save your daughter from having to do later. Every time my sons sigh with annoyance about having to do a chore, I think about their future partnerships. If you have children, halting the patriarchal practice of treating boys like 'gods' is one of your most important contributions to the world.

It is time for a re-ordering of the world as we know it—built on the foundations of love and joy. As Monica Sjöö and Barbara Mor wrote:

"The patriarchal God has only one commandment:
Punish life for being what it is.
The Goddess also has only one commandment:
Love life, for it is what it is."[15]

---

[15] Sjöö, Monica and Mor, Barbara. *The Great Cosmic Mother: Rediscovering the Religion of the Earth*. HarperOne; 2nd edition, 1987.

Focus on What You *Can* Control

Let's face it, there are a myriad of structural inequalities that are completely out of our control. Focus on what you can control or change first. Since the one person we *can* change is ourselves, we will begin there—and then work toward toppling the system itself.

This book contains suggestions that worked for me—but I realize that not everything will work for everyone. Use the Al-Anon suggestion: "Take what you like and leave the rest!"

You don't have to do everything all at once. It is enough to *decide* that you want to do it. When the time comes to do it, you will know it, and will have the strength and energy to do so. But it is important to start *somewhere,* or you will never get anywhere. As Angela Davis once wrote, "I am no longer accepting the things I cannot change. I am changing the things I cannot accept."

You may be starting with a very low energy level, and that is more than OK. Just the fact that you are reading this book in a world where fewer and fewer people read is a small miracle! Give yourself some credit.

There have been years where I have barely moved from my bed to the couch on a given day. As women, we are taught to push and push at our own detriment. Just do what you can every day.

That is enough.

3 Options

If you don't like something about yourself, you generally have 3 options—you can continue to despise that part of yourself, you can change it, or you can accept it.

I recently read a book—that I wouldn't really recommend as feminist, but I enjoyed nonetheless—called *UnFu*k Yourself*.[16] I have always adored blunt people, and this Scottish dude really nailed some things on the head for me. He gave an analogy about someone who was struggling with their weight—and that alone was playing all sorts of mind games with their self-worth. The simple strategy of just accepting the fact that they did not want to stop eating junk food or to do the exercise required to maintain the weight they easily maintained when they were younger was all that it took for this person to get 'unfu*ked.'

That struck a chord with me—even though the male version of this is likely more simplified than it is for us as females. I don't eat much junk food, and I have never been on a diet or struggled significantly with my weight. However, after my surgery, my stomach is less than my favorite part of my body—complete with a long scar running the length of my belly, stretch marks from 2 births and the extra bit of padding I have put on after 40.

After absorbing the author's bluntness, I was like, *OK, he is right.* I have no intention of going on a diet—not now or ever—and I am not likely to start running marathons or to take up weight lifting. There is also no way I am doing any sort of cosmetic surgery to change how my stomach looks or to lessen the severity of the scar. *Am I really going to spend the rest of my life being upset by a stomach that the majority of women on our planet also share to some degree?*

---

[16] Bishop, Gary John. *Unfu*k Yourself: Get Out of Your Head and into Your Life*. HarperOne; 2017.

This is where awesome art by women comes in—and why I have paintings by Elisabeth Slettnes, Arna Baartz, Lucy Pierce, Jakki Moore and others hung throughout my home. In a photo-shopped world, women need regular reminders of what most of us *actually* look like![17]

In any case, my stomach is under acceptance and I am doing a better job of dressing myself so that I feel happy with it—i.e., anything tight is going in the Goodwill box and I am going to stop wearing black every day to mask my body. My colorful friend Vigdis even sent me a fun catalog from Gudrun Sjödén to inspire me to get started.

The fact is that even when I was younger, I never thought my stomach was good enough, flat enough, or fit enough—and I had a big mole on it to boot! *How many women feel bad about this?* As Anita A. Johnston wrote, "Why has a naturally masculine shape (broad shoulders, no waist, narrow hips, flat belly) become the ideal for the female body? Why is it that those aspects of a woman's body that are most closely related to her innate female power, the capacity of her belly, hips, and thighs to carry and sustain life, are diminished in our society's version of a beautiful woman?"[18]

Back to your 3 options... they apply to more than just your stomach. These options apply to *all* of your life. Don't waste a moment hating something about yourself—especially if you are measuring by the standards of Capitalist Patriarchy.

Define your own standards and edit your life accordingly.

---

[17] If you need a little belly pick-me-up yourself, check out 'Belly Love' by glasmond.

[18] Johnson, Anita A. PhD. *Eating in the Light of the Moon: How Women Can Transform Their Relationship with Food Through Myths, Metaphors, and Storytelling.* Gurze Books; 2000.

Identify Your Life-Affirming and Life-Depleting Habits

Make a list of all your life-affirming and life-depleting habits. There is no blame or judgment here—just write the first things that come to your mind. Many of us are socialized to do things without thinking about whether they are in our best interest or not. Gabor Maté wrote that,

> "In order to heal, it is essential to gather the strength to think negatively. Negative thinking is not a doleful, pessimistic view that masquerades as "realism." Rather, it is a willingness to consider what is not working. What is not in balance? What have I ignored? What is my body saying no to? Without these questions, the stresses responsible for our lack of balance will remain hidden."[19]

So, be honest with yourself and write it all out. On the left, list all the things you do that are either getting in the way of the life you want—or outright destroying it. This could be things like eating entire bags of chips in one sitting, drinking too much alcohol, not exercising, doing all the housework by yourself, etc.

On the right, list all the things you do that make you feel really great. This might include things like cuddling with your dog, taking long walks, juicing every day, etc.

Christiane Northrup wrote, "All of us are given a certain amount of crap to compost. Get it out of you so that you can mix it into rich soil and create something new. Learn from it, write a poem expressing it, and dance or cry it out of you to heal yourself.

---

[19] Maté, Gabor. *When the Body Says No: Understanding the Stress-Disease Connection.* Wiley; 2011.

Create something better from the crap so that it doesn't define your life or make you sick."[20]

I wholeheartedly agree! List-making is one tool that helps me stay on track. Decide what is working for you and what is not. Acknowledging these patterns is the first step. Then you can begin to add and delete things from your life.

This is an ongoing list—one that you could potentially work on for a year or more before starting a new one. Just like weeding a garden, our lives need constant pruning. The habits we form in childhood and early adulthood are often not the same ones that will serve us well later in life.

When you begin to take care of yourself better and begin to heal, your life-depleting habits will also become less appealing. I have come to believe that many women drink excessively (or stress eat) because their lives are far from ideal. As females, many of us are not taught to take care of ourselves. We are groomed to take care of everyone else first—which often leaves us with very little for ourselves. So, we take the few scraps we are given and become malnourished. When we begin to flip this paradigm, everything changes. We are re-charged and transformed.

---

[20] Northrup, Christiane. *Goddesses Never Age: The Secret Prescription for Radiance, Vitality, and Well-Being.* Hay House; 2018.

Identify What You Love and What You Hate

One author who really helped me with her fun crayon-colored workbooks is SARK, who has that magical ability to help bring dreams out of our subconscious minds and into the world. She wrote, "Don't step into lives that aren't yours, make choices that aren't nourishing, or dance stiffly for years with the wrong partner, or parts of yourself."[21]

Spot on. Let's begin to identify these things. Make a list of all the things in your life that you love and hate.

On the left, make a list of all the people, places, things and activities that you hate. Could be your abusive father-in-law, going to awkward family dinners, your current job, etc.

On the right, list all the things in your life that you absolutely love —like going to the beach, keeping a journal, eating a fresh avocado, etc. Note that none of these items need to cost money to start with. When I was broke, going to the library and getting stacks of books was my starting point. I owe my current happiness to that habit.

What we are aiming for is lives filled with things that we absolutely love, while reducing or eliminating anything we hate.

Note that patriarchy is still (currently) an issue for women everywhere—but if we all add patriarchy on the left, we will slowly (or, perhaps swiftly) cross that off too! The same goes for capitalism. I believe in thinking BIG! When we begin to do so collectively, the world will shift enormously.

---

[21] SARK. *Succulent Wild Woman: Dancing with your Wonder-full Self!* Simon Schuster; 1997.

Work Through Childhood Trauma

I have tried to structure the chapters in relative order, but this was a tough one to decide where to place. It seems to me that you can't get anywhere without addressing this somewhere near the beginning.

I have worked through past trauma many times—each time believing I was "done" with *that*—only to have it come up on a deeper level later. As Laura Davis wrote, "The healing process is best described as a spiral. Survivors go through the stages once, sometimes many times; sometimes in one order, sometimes in another. Each time they hit a stage again, they move up the spiral: they can integrate new information and a broader range of feelings, utilize more resources, take better care of themselves, and make deeper changes."[22]

If you did not have the best childhood, it may be difficult for you to form healthy habits—even as an adult. Even if you did have a so-called "healthy" childhood, many of the ways females are raised during their young years encourage meekness and subordination.

It is important to work through your "stuff" because it won't go away on its own—and it is common for many of us to self-sabotage.

I think we must also begin to understand the collective trauma of sexual abuse in the context of keeping women down. Andrea Dworkin wrote long ago that, "We need to understand what sexual abuse has done to us—why are we so damned hard to organize? We need to comprehend that sexual abuse has broken us into a million pieces and we carry those pieces bumping and crashing inside: we're broken rock inside; chaos; afraid and unsure

---

[22] Davis, Laura. *Allies in Healing.* HarperCollins Publishers; 2012.

when not cold and numb. We're heroes at endurance; but so far cowards at resistance."[23] This is one reason I believe that focusing on our individual healing from such abuse is so critical. We can learn to place blame and shame back with the perpetrator, as Jane Caputi discusses in her brilliant paper, "Take back what doesn't belong to me."[24]

If you are healing from sexual abuse or rape, Annie Finch has an amazing ritual available online.[25] If you are a fellow sexual abuse survivor, I send you my warmest and biggest embrace. Working through this trauma has been one of the hardest things I have ever done. *But it was worth it.* As Annie wrote in her post:

> "Unfortunately for those of us who have experienced sexual abuse, it seems pretty clear that ignoring such an experience, no matter how long you ignore it, cannot make it go away. The repressed memories of times when you disassociated from your body and denied your emotions can drain away at your energy for years or decades. Healing from sexual abuse is essential work if we aim to live our lives fully, to share our gifts completely. The good news is that, as those of us who are in the midst of the healing process already know, healing is possible and can be quite a simple process."

I have had to fight really hard to establish good habits for myself. And even sometimes when I did, they would slip by the wayside once the inevitable drama came up. For most of my life, there was

---

23 Dworkin, Andrea. *Life and Death*. Free Press; 1997.
24 Caputi, Jane. "Take back what doesn't belong to me": sexual violence, resistance and the "transmission of affect." Women's Studies International Forum, Vol. 26, No. 1, pp. 1–14, 2003. Copyright 2002 Elsevier Science Ltd.
25 Finch, Annie. "Sexual Abuse Healing Ritual." http://anniefinch.com/ritual-healing-sexual/

always drama. Because I was used to it—or some would say, even addicted to it. It was *familiar.* When there wasn't drama, I would create it. As Lucy Pearce wrote in *Burning Woman*, "As the daughters of patriarchy, many of us have lived in trauma as our default our whole lives."[26]

In fact, some of us might not know what to do with good things (or people) that come into our lives. It may take time to heal before we can allow joy into our lives.

As I became healthier, I became allergic to drama and learned how to avoid it. The investment in time we spend on healing our lives will be repaid ten-fold. As Dr. Christiane Northrup writes, "Every woman who heals herself helps heal all the women who came before her and all those who will come after."[27]

It may be that it takes birthing our children to inspire some of us to heal. Until I became pregnant with my son, I did not realize how critically important it was for me to heal. I just did not value myself. But, when I thought about that tiny, innocent little baby growing inside me, I wanted a completely different life for him. While, perhaps, I may have come to that conclusion later in life without children, I am not certain of that. In fact, it seems unlikely. When the indoctrination is deep, I think it sometimes takes something outside of ourselves to begin the process—although it could also include giving birth to a project or something larger than ourselves.

This is another reason inner-child work can be very effective. I often think about 'little Trista' as a small child and hold her in my heart. I have learned to speak to her with love and compassion— the way I speak to my own children.

---

[26] Pearce, Lucy. *Burning Woman.* Womancraft Publishing; 2016.
[27] Northrup, Christiane M.D. *Mother-Daughter Wisdom: Creating a Legacy of Physical and Emotional Health.* Bantam; 2005.

The insidious thing about abuse is that it teaches you to continue to mistreat yourself long after the abuser is out of your life—so you are effectively continuing to do his work for him. For most of my life, I spoke to myself horribly. When I decided that I must stop doing that, my life began to change enormously. While I still slip on occasion, I try to treat myself with loving kindness now—and have filled my life with people who do the same.

Take a moment and think about what that would look and feel like for you. Even if you just stopped here, healing your childhood trauma would make ripples across the entire world.

Whatever your path, I hope you know that you deserve to find healing.[28]

---

[28] Irene Lyon's work has been helpful to me. Check out her YouTube channel, particularly these videos: "The burden of childhood trauma and how to lift it" and "How to come out of a chronic freeze response after repeated stress & trauma."

Evaluate All Relationships

Your most important relationship is the one you have with yourself. So, make sure you are treating yourself well and keeping the promises you make. If you don't have that down pretty well, any other relationship will be a bit challenging. You can't live well if you have a guilty conscience. So, do your best to live with integrity, following the principles you believe in. If you know you are betraying yourself in an area, work on amending that. Patricia Lynn Reilly has an excellent book about making vows to your self —which I strongly recommend if you are feeling weak in this area.[29]

The second most critical relationship is that with your partner, if you have one. Make sure you are spending your life with someone you want to spend it with. If you hate your partner, you are going to hate your life. Nothing else can make up for a shitty partner.

It is my belief that we should live with people who make our lives easier, not more difficult. Most women are taught that their worth is in being partnered with someone who will make them "whole." The truth is that a lot of these guys[30] just end up depleting us further and we become far less than even half a person.

Women are often groomed to set the bar too low. Looking back at some of my previous relationships, I can see how far I have come. I would never put up with the nonsense I did in my earlier years.

---

[29] Reilly, Patricia Lynn. *I Promise Myself: Making a Commitment to Yourself and Your Dreams*. Conari Press; 2000.

[30] I write 'guys' as a generalization. I am bi-sexual and currently partnered in a monogamous relationship with a man. I hope it goes without saying that *any* shitty or abusive relationship is not worth your time or energy.

This quote from Don Miguel Ruiz really helped me to see things more clearly.

> "How can someone tell you, 'I love you,' and then mistreat you and abuse you, humiliate you, and disrespect you? That person may claim to love you, but is it really love? If we love, we want the best for those we love."[31]

Life is hard enough as it is—you don't need your primary relationship to make it harder. So, take a good look at your partner, and determine honestly whether the relationship can be repaired if it is lacking or broken.[32]

> "If it works, keep going. If it doesn't work, then do yourself and your partner a favor: walk way; let her go. Don't be selfish. Give your partner the opportunity to find what she really wants, and at the same time, give yourself the opportunity. If it's not going to work, it is better to look in a different direction. If you cannot love your partner the way she is, someone else can love her just as she is. Don't waste your time, and don't waste your partner's time. This is respect."[33]

Next, begin to look at your other relationships with family and friends. Be relentless. No one is off the table, except for minor children—not your patriarchal father who only loves you when

---

[31] Ruiz, Don Miguel. *The Mastery of Love: A Practical Guide to the Art of Relationship: A Toltec Wisdom Book.* Amber-Allen Publishing; 1999.

[32] Please note, If you are just beginning to do any sort of work regarding healing sexual abuse, take at least a year before making any sort of relationship decisions. Unless your relationship is toxic or abusive, you will need some time to begin to process before you will be in a position to make big life decisions.

[33] Ruiz, Don Miguel. *The Mastery of Love: A Practical Guide to the Art of Relationship: A Toltec Wisdom Book.* Amber-Allen Publishing; 1999.

you do as you are told or childhood best friend who not-so-secretly likes you better when times are hard. Sometimes healing involves walking away—sometimes it is working through things. You will know what is right when you listen to your gut.

Don't spend one minute of your precious life-energy on anyone who doesn't deserve it. I could write several books on all the time I have wasted on assholes—but then I would just be wasting more of my life!

The best thing to do in this situation is to walk away and learn how to live an amazing life without them. There are some people who literally get off on causing other people pain. Don't feed into their energy. As bell hooks wrote, "All too often women believe it is a sign of commitment, an expression of love, to endure unkindness or cruelty, to forgive and forget. In actuality, when we love rightly we know that the healthy, loving response to cruelty and abuse is putting ourselves out of harm's way."[34]

If someone does not treat you like the Queen that you are, move along. No explanation necessary.

---

[34] hooks, bell. *All About Love: New Visions*. William Morrow; 1999.

Embrace Failure

As you read through this book, you will notice that my life is far from perfect. But I try to enjoy every day. Some days are still duds, and I let myself read, watch a show or just do nothing—and start fresh the next day.

One thing I learned from my time in Lebanon several decades ago is that happiness is often a choice. My first husband's family is filled with happy and loving people, despite enduring years of war and living through what most of us would probably consider hell. His family is among the healthiest I have ever met. And if you know traditional Lebanese families, you know they are LARGE! I believe the reason for this is their strong sense of family and community.

I have been divorced two times—and had dozens of other relationships and projects fail. But who cares?

And I am *horrible* at speaking Norwegian—despite my best efforts. I spent so long being embarrassed about my bad Norwegian. Now I have a really cool crone-ish teacher who just sighs at my poor pronunciation emphatically with a big smile, laughs—and occasionally yells and beats her hand on the table with frustration, "TRISTA!!!!!"

One day, my Norwegian will be *better.* But it will likely never be perfect. I will likely always have a very strong American accent and mispronounce things, even when I do get the grammar right.

Living in another country with another language gives you humility—but it also gives you perspective and challenges your deepest assumptions.

There is no one "right" way across all cultures. We can learn a bit from each. My American perspective was largely influenced by both Lebanese and Norwegian culture—and my love for reading promiscuously. Use reading books as a way to learn from the mistakes of others—and show yourself grace when you do things less than perfectly.

Oftentimes, you can turn a 'failure' into a win. My first husband remains one of the most important people in my life. Our marriage did not work, but he has become the big brother I never had—offering unconditional love and support in a way I always longed for. He has been one of my biggest fans, and proudly displays many of my books in his living room to show off when he has guests. We have become family and support systems for each other and our children. He will always be "Uncle Hussein" to my children—who still can't imagine that we were a married couple 24 years ago! If you had told me this would happen two decades ago, I never would have believed it. At that time, I never thought I could live my life without him. And that is still true to some extent. We just had to find a way to still stay closely connected without driving each other nuts!

Some relationships are worth fighting for, even if you have to give up the dreams you envisioned for them. Sometimes our failures provide more blessings than our dreams.

Limit Time on Social Media

We all have our days where Capitalist Patriarchy drains us dry and makes us feel hopeless. Always allow yourself the mental health days you need. But don't move in there. If you're at your wits end, stop everything and go for a walk.

You can't live your best life online.

You are also unlikely to find solutions there.

The internet is filled with trolls—often there just there specifically to annoy feminists. *Don't feed them.*

When I stopped spending so much time on social media, I began to read a book a day on average. That might seem excessive, but I am a speed reader. If you read regularly, your reading speed will improve and you will be able to read and absorb more than you ever thought possible. In addition, you will not feel as fragmented as you do reading on the internet, skimming from one thing to another. You also will not feel depleted from the constant fighting online.

The internet has its purposes, but it cannot replace real life.

Invest in yourself by reading and meditating every day. Don't waste time reading endless articles on Facebook everyday about how bad things are. There are *always* bad things happening. That doesn't mean you turn your back on people who need your help. But what good does reading endless articles about this accomplish? Not a lot. You could spend your entire life reading about bad things every single day. It would change nothing. We must ACT. That begins with you—ensuring that you are in a position to actually help where you are needed.

One reason I believe things have not changed enough for females is because we have not been allowed time to heal and become strong. Social media is another means of robbing us of our valuable time via its endless distractions.

Live Within Your Means

As a mortgage broker, I saw many people who wanted to stretch their housing budget w-a-y too far. Mortgage standards have stretched themselves. It used to be that you'd get a 10- or 15-year loan. Then the 30-year became standard. In my entire 13-year career, despite my advice to nearly every client, I only did two 15-year loans—and one of them was for my father. When I left the industry, they were stretching out loans 40- and 50-years.

When you examine an amortization schedule, you see that you pay more interest upfront, and only barely begin to pay down a 30-year loan after about year 5. The bulk of the loan is paid down at the end. The bank takes their money first. This is why frequent refinancing and longer loan terms are not your friends. I recommend spending no more than 28% of your income on housing.

Housing costs have gone up and sometimes people say that it's not possible to pay so little for housing. But there is always a way to save more money. A few ideas: tiny houses, get a roommate or get rid of your car.

If you have a mortgage, pay it off as soon as possible. One of my goals is to be mortgage-free as soon as possible. Given that I had to start over in mid-life, this will take some creativity, but I do believe it can be done. If you make an extra mortgage payment every year, you will shave 7 years off your mortgage.

There are also lots of creative shows out there that can give you ideas. One of my favorites is *How to Live Mortgage Free* with Sarah Beeny. It also has given me a lot of ideas about inexpensive repairs to our home that we can do ourselves. I believe we are much more self-reliant than we give ourselves credit for.

After my divorce, I shared a big house with a single dad and his 4 kids. It was colorful to have 6 children in the house—and as many as 9 when my soon-to-be stepsons came to visit while my roommate's niece was also visiting—but it worked. It's also nice as a single parent to have another caring adult in the house. After that, my mother lived with us, which worked out even better. The kids still miss having Grandma around. In my own life, my mother has been a life-saver. I would not have made it during my years as a single mom without her.

I am a big proponent of shared housing—especially for those trying to get back on their feet. As James Baldwin wrote, "Anyone who has ever struggled with poverty knows how extremely expensive it is to be poor." One thing I saw over and over again as a broker is that the poor are further disadvantaged by the banking system—while the rich are rewarded by it. Sharing costs with other responsible adults is one way to get around this. When you pool your resources together, you broaden your options.

There is almost nothing worse than financial stress in my opinion. If you stretch your housing budget too far, you will be stressed out every single month. *Don't do this to yourself!*

Same goes for credit cards. Yes, sometimes it seems like they are the only option, but there are usually other options. The greatest loss we suffer from lack of community is not being able to count on our tribe to help us out.

Going back to my Lebanese family... they help each other! They live near each other and often eat together. They take turns hosting and bringing their specialty dishes.[35] If someone is sick,

---

[35] While it is true that, for the most part, this family is traditional, I did not observe them as patriarchal in the traditionally negative sense—nor are they driven by capitalist values. Sadly, I feel I have to include this footnote, because on almost every occasion that I mention I was married to an Arab, the assumption is usually that I was treated poorly by either my husband or

they are brought food. If someone needs money, they can count on family to help them. We can stretch our dollars farther working together.

If your family of origin is not close or helpful, form your own tribe. If you do not have a monthly and yearly budget, take some time to make one. There are many resources online that can help if you don't know where to start—or check out the suggested reading at the end of this book. For most of us, there is not currently a way to get around managing money—so we may as well learn how to do it in ways that serve us.

We can't take down a system we know nothing about. So it behooves us to learn as much as we can, so that we can figure out creative strategies to live well in the meantime—and eventually knock it down altogether.

---

his family. That was never the case. I go to into this in more detail in *Hearts Aren't Made of Glass* and *Jesus, Muhammad and the Goddess*.

Realize You Are Not Your Financial Status

As I mentioned, I have lived at nearly all fringes of the wealth and poverty rainbow. It is possible (although admittedly more difficult) to be happy whatever your current financial status.

For years, I had a lot of shame about my credit score, which tanked as a result of my former husband's addictions and the careless choices that were fueled by them.

When I came to Norway, those same feelings of inadequacy followed me, so much that I didn't even think about purchasing a home—even when I finally had a down payment to do so. I avoided the bank like the plague and had to build up my courage even to go in and talk to someone there.

I was shocked to find out that my bad credit did not follow me here. In fact, I was told I have quite good credit!! The standards by which they rate this are quite different here than they are in the United States, which could be an entire book by itself—but what I mean to tell you is *don't judge yourself by a totally arbitrary number.*

A credit score is only a picture in time. It is never static, and you can work to improve it. I spent 12 years helping hundreds of people improve their credit and then my credit was tanked by someone else in the blink of an eye.

I really liked what Kate Northrup had to say about this:

> "Before you start feeling bad about yourself for your debt, this would be a good moment to remind yourself that money doesn't exist—it's just a system of value exchange. That's it. Pure and simple. So, if you have debt, you've received value and you've not given the equivalent value back to the particular party in the exchange yet. That's all it means. It doesn't mean you're a bad person. It doesn't

mean you're a screwup. You're not hopeless. You're not a mess. You simply have more value to give."[36]

I used to think credit was an indication of character, and it sometimes is. However, over the years I also found that many people were hit by forces they could not control. Don't base your self-worth on your credit score or how much money you currently have. You are so much more than that.

---

[36] Northrup, Kate. *Money, A Love Story: Untangling Your Finances, Creating the Life You Really Want, and Living Your Purpose.* Hay House Inc.; 2013.

Don't Buy into Patriarchal Beauty Standards

Many of the beauty products we use are slowly killing us without our knowledge or explicit consent. While I identify strongly as a feminist, it is still hard to part with the privilege of being considered "pretty." As I grow older, I am beginning to calculate what pretty costs.

At 37, I dyed my hair for what I promised myself would be the last time. If you research the negative effects of hair dye, it is not something you would willingly use on any part of your body.

And then we digress to the issue of body hair; I won't go into pubic hair because that seems to be discussed everywhere lately. Underarm hair seems to carry even more of a taboo, likely because it is more visible.

For years, I maintained the ritual shaving and putting on deodorant each morning, knowing that it was not good for me.

All of that came to an end when my six-year-old daughter stopped me while I was putting on my usual brand and asked when she would start to wear deodorant.

I told her, "Hopefully never, it's poison."

She asked, "Then why do *you* wear it, Mommy?"

I promised her I would stop. She looked me dead in the eye and demanded to know, "When?" That was it for me.

The indoctrination begins early; it starts with those of us who are mothers. Our daughters watch our every move, how we treat ourselves. I realize now I failed my daughter in some ways, by going along with a system that I didn't even believe in. Why is how other people perceive us more important than how we *feel*? Is looking and smelling "good" more important than that?

At one point, I had to ask myself, 'Am I *really* spending all this time trying to eat healthy, organic food only to ingest toxins via my personal care products?'

The same toxins that we are absorbing into our bodies are often made in poor countries, bringing disastrous consequences for the local environment as well as the individual health of millions of inhabitants. As Kathleen Dean Moore stated, "We believe we can destroy our habitat without also destroying ourselves. How could we be so tragically wrong?"[37]

You can't do something to/for yourself that simultaneously hurts another being without an additional adverse effect. So *why* do we continue to buy into a system that hurts women everywhere?

And here is one more thing to consider: In a world where we don't think our choices matter, they can. Consider the cost of grooming your hair. The average American woman will spend over $55,000 over the course of her lifetime on her hair.[38] How many women die completely broke? (The answer is more than half of us!)

Whenever I post about this on social media, it always becomes divisive, so here is where I will leave it. Shaving or not shaving—or wearing or not wearing makeup or deodorant—does not make you less or more of a feminist. Sometimes I still shave if I get a wild hair. I sometimes wear makeup, especially when I am feeling really tired and want a little pick-me-up. It is more about how *I*

---

[37] Democker, Mary. "If Your House Is On Fire: Kathleen Dean Moore On The Moral Urgency Of Climate Change." *The Sun*, December 2012.

[38] Furguson, Sarah. "How Expensive is Your Hair?" *DailyMail*; June 23, 2017.

feel. My children, interestingly enough, hate it when I wear makeup. My husband doesn't notice one way or another. But I don't spend money on makeup or shaving. I rarely purchase it— maybe a lipstick every 5 years and an occasional tube of mascara. As with any purchase, I am very intentional about how I will spend my money.

The way we groom our hair is probably not a life-changing event for most of us, but that small everyday choice can have an economic impact on our net worth. It can also change what we can afford to contribute to the world at large. Riane Eisler stated: "Women represent 70 percent of the 1.3 billion people in our world who live in absolute poverty. Consequently, as Joan Holmes, president of the Hunger Project, points out, any realistic efforts to change patterns of chronic hunger and poverty require changing traditions of discrimination against women."[39]

When we give up the idea that our primary importance is based on how we look, we stop buying all the makeup, hair products, new clothes, etc. that can cost us thousands of dollars every year. We are talking about a $7 billion-dollar-a-year industry in the United States alone that profits from women feeling bad about themselves. That is a serious amount of money that could change a lot for females worldwide.

I don't spend money on most of that any more. I spend any extra money I have on supporting women's projects, books and CD's— or reinvesting in my own projects. As Lucy Pearce notes, "Society INVESTS in us hating ourselves, one of the most powerful ways to stick it to the system is to decide that's just not an option, that hate is a waste of time and you've got bigger things to do."[40]

---

[39] Eisler, Riane. *The Real Wealth of Nations*. Berrett-Koehler Publishers; 2008.
[40] Pearce, Lucy. *Burning Woman*. Womancraft Publishing; 2016.

I don't want to continue to support a system where women are sliced and diced on Photoshop and still only make 77 cents on the dollar. As women, we cannot afford to support beauty expectations that harm us both collectively and individually.

Ditch Your Car

My reformation from country club princess to granola mama didn't happen all at once. I had been slowly evolving for a while, but things changed drastically for me when I met Anders and experienced his culture in Norway.

As with most travel and exposure to other cultures, it's what I noticed about what we took for granted as "normal" here that opened my eyes the most. I didn't realize how badly we denigrated those who don't drive cars in the U.S. until I re-watched *The 40-Year-Old Virgin* with Anders. While I still find that movie hysterical, it is interesting social commentary that the nerdy virgin rides a bike.

Anders noticed it right off the bat. "Men who don't drive cars here are really treated like losers aren't they?"

I realized he was right. How many times are people completely identified with their cars? How many times has a woman turned down a nice guy because she didn't like what he was driving? And how do men complete the role of "man" if they cannot pick up a woman for a date?

Let's be honest: *It does seem weird*. We take it for granted in the U.S. that people *own* cars. And the richer they are, the nicer that car should be. The owning part of that usually means they have *financed* a car—or rather, that they're indebted to someone else for their *sense of self*.

On my first trip to Norway, it was wet and rainy every day. We traveled by foot, bus or train. Every excursion required that we walk at least 10 minutes up or down a steep hill. I saw many people of all ages walking up and down the hill all day long, many carrying heavy bags of groceries. *It wasn't so bad*. I got used to the rain and the exercise felt good throughout the day.

I have always believed that you *had* to have a car. My second husband was a high-end car dealer for most of our marriage. Seeing how people lived in Norway was the first time I actually stopped and thought about whether having a car was *necessary*.

When I came home, I decided to sell my car.

In the suburban community I previously lived in, it would have been nearly impossible to live without a car, so I eased into it.

During the transition, I got used to walking more. In the suburbs, when you walk, people assume you must be having car problems. I can't tell you how many times a friend stopped, worried that my car had broken down. While I appreciated the sentiment, I found it quite amusing!

I decided to move back to a flatter, more urban part of Portland where I could walk nearly everywhere. I sold more than half my belongings and moved into a smaller space we shared with another family. We walked to and from school every day, stopping on the way home for groceries. It was easier than I ever thought it could be.

Americans spend an average of 75 minutes a day in their cars—but I always hated driving. It made me tired and cranky to sit in traffic. I now spend an average of 75 minutes a day walking, which means I'm in fairly good shape without a gym membership.

When I need to go somewhere distant, I take public transport. On some occasions, I borrow a vehicle—but that's more and more uncommon. I have also used Uber and Zipcar at times, which gave me a few more options.

I have now spent more than 7 years without a car, and I rarely miss it.

I have not done all the math, but I know I have saved tens of thousands of dollars every single year. I don't have insurance, car payments or gas and maintenance expenses. And, I'm in a good mood from all the daily exercise I get. I don't plan to own a car again. This frees up quite a bit of money for other things that are more important to me.

I know many people will find the thought of not owning a car practically insane. But consider this: *Driving a car is the most air polluting act an average citizen commits.*[41]

If you cannot fathom life without a car, at least consider driving less if you are able-bodied. You will save money, gain health and stop participating in the destruction of Mother Earth.

---

[41] Gislason, Stephen MD. *The Environment.* Alpha Nutrition; 2017.

Forget Your Phone

For years, I wanted to get rid of my phone—but I didn't think I could. I spent over 3 years without a telephone and here is what I learned.

Over the years, I had developed an unhealthy dependence on my phone. I often woke in the night to check messages. I looked at it first thing in the morning and the last thing before going to bed.

I felt a certain nervousness and neediness around my phone. I felt indebted to it somehow. On one hand, I hated the phone. On the other, I felt it was necessary. I was certain my friends and family had to be able to reach me at all times. Ironically, when I told my closest friends and family, none of them seemed devastated, or even surprised by my decision.

When I began to learn about the dark side of Smartphones, I became increasingly uncomfortable with my use of this device. I decided to get rid of my phone after reading Raffi Cavoukian's book, *Lightweb Darkweb*.

The book takes you through the downfalls of both social media and Smartphones, addressing everything from sustainability to the ill-effects of radiation on children. This got to me: "Would you want your son or daughter working 12-hour shifts for next to nothing, doing mind-numbing, repetitive tasks for weeks and months on end, and living in cramped, multiple-story lodgings draped with suicide-prevention netting? If not, ask yourself: How do I feel about my infatuation with the digital devices that come from such hard labour and brutal conditions?"[42]

---

[42] Cavoukian, Raffi. *Lightweb Darkweb: Three Reasons to Reform Social Media Before It Reforms Us.* Homeland Pr; 2013.

We can and should certainly call on cell phone companies to use better practices, but we have no assurances that they will. I don't have high hopes for any major corporations at this point in time. Recycling phones does very little to help. According to *Mother Jones:* "Only 11 percent of phones and other mobile devices are ever even collected. What programs do exist often amount to shipping old phones and TVs to Chinese villages, where they are broken up and bathed in acid to remove gold and silver—resulting in terrible lead and dioxin pollution."[43]

My point is that we are brainwashed into buying products that don't serve us well, individually or collectively. Many of these items come at a very high cost to others who don't have the luxury of shipping their toxic waste off somewhere else. My hope is people will begin to challenge what items are deemed "necessary."

I also did not realize how fragmenting it is to be looking at your cell phone all day until I got rid of mine. I knew on some level that my days were being chopped up, but I did not fully comprehend just how distracting a phone can be. Calls, texts, emails... the constant need to check all three *and* Facebook *and* Twitter. The Smartphone interrupts your ability to think. All. Day. Long.

I was at least three times as productive after I got rid of my phone. And while I did eventually revert to using a phone again, I will never use it again in the same way. My phone is used very sparingly. I keep it as far away as possible from me most of the day. Being acutely aware of the health risks—my phone is a tool for me to use when I need it, not the other way around. Nicolas Pineault recently wrote:

---

[43]   Butler, Kiera. "Your Smartphone's Dirty, Radioactive Secret." *Mother Jones*, November 2012.

"You should NEVER use a cell phone right next to your head—unless you couldn't care less about getting brain cancer." That's not me saying it. This is what Consumer Reports has been recommending to all of their readers since early 2016. Unless it's on 'Airplane Mode' or completely powered off, your phone is constantly emitting radiation as it tries to connect to a 4G/LTE cellular network, to a WiFi network, or to a Bluetooth device. So essentially, what you're doing when you keep your phone in your pocket all day is you're slowly but surely "frying" your reproductive organs."[44]

I am very careful about cell phone use for both myself and my children.

Cell phones can also be a waste of our life energy. As Jim Kwik has said, "When you wake up in the morning and immediately check social media, you're training yourself to be reactive. You sell your sovereignty to the world if you start by checking your phone first thing in the morning."

Lastly, when you are with friends and family, please put your phone away. So often I see people out to eat who are both on their phones, completely ignoring each other! There are very few things I am strict on in regards to manners, but this is just rude. We do not allow phones at our dinner table and I would never even think of pulling my phone out while I was with a friend unless there was an emergency.

Much like an occasional pause from alcohol can be illuminating, I advocate taking a break from your phone at times to see what the benefits are for you.

---

[44] Pineault, Nicolas. "3 Ways To Use Your Phone WITHOUT ZAPPING YOUR HEALTH." *EMF Summit*. N&G Média Inc.; 2017.

Buy, Trade or Borrow Used Clothing

One of the most destructive things we do to the environment—and ourselves[45]—is to buy new clothing. Much of it is produced with micro-fibers now, which shed every time we wash our clothes and then make their way into our food.[46] Not to mention that a large percentage of clothing is produced in sweatshops, under horrible conditions for the people working there—basically as slaves.[47] I don't believe we can walk around in clothing manufactured like this and not have it affect us negatively.

One thing you can do to help is to buy or trade used clothing—which will also save you a considerable amount of money. I had a friend who loved to go to thrift shops and had a real knack for getting amazing clothes for almost nothing. The trick is to not buy more than what you need.

I am more of a minimalist, but I love Marie Kondō—and have received a lot of inspiration from her work.[48] Since I had already discarded much of my clothing, her advice about clothing was irrelevant to me. But one thing I realized after reading her book is that I really did not have much of anything clothes-wise that sparked *joy*.

I think this is something I have missed out on. When I was broke, I got into the habit of taking whatever was given to me and wearing the first thing I could grab from the closet. I am still a fan of buying used—but going forward, I will be spending more time on finding clothing that I absolutely love. I believe we can begin to dress in a way that is infused with both integrity and joy.

---

[45] Zaroff, Marci. "Is Your Clothing Toxic?" Goop.com
[46] Mercola, Dr. Joseph "Major Plastic Problems in Oceans From Clothes." Mercola.com; February 20, 2019.
[47] I highly recommend the documentary, *The True Cost.* https://truecostmovie
[48] Kondō, Marie *The Life-Changing Magic of Tidying Up: The Japanese Art of Decluttering and Organizing.* Ten Speed Press; 2014.

Take Loving Your Body to the Next Level

I have been working toward loving my body for a while now, but it is a process for me. Recently I picked up a book that was sort of woo-woo for me, but it hooked me—*Liver Rescue*. I had been working through a variety of health problems over the past year and but remained sluggish. In reading this book, I learned that most of us have compromised livers and can't really afford to eat and drink like our parents and grandparents did—due to environmental and other toxins. I committed to a total cleanse and quickly felt much better than I had in years.

This is paraphrased, but one of the things he wrote that really got to me was—*if you knew how much your liver did for you, you would really love her and take care of her*. He describes the liver as our "greatest ally, the one that's been there for you all this time, the one working harder than anyone knows."[49] I loved the way he depicted our organs as friends and family members.

It got me thinking that we really ought to be thinking about loving our bodies internally—instead of focusing so much on how they look from the outside. I have begun to think along these lines and it makes a profound difference in what I am willing to ingest. Sonia Johnson wrote, "To the extent that we can act as if we love our bodies, we create the essential and unique physical power we are here on the planet now to share with Earth's body. Until we take our own bodies seriously, we cannot truthfully say we care about hers or anyone else's, and we will be unable to help as we otherwise could when we are most needed."[50]

---

[49] William, Anthony. *Medical Medium Liver Rescue: Answers to Eczema, Psoriasis, Diabetes, Strep, Acne, Gout, Bloating, Gallstones, Adrenal Stress, Fatigue, Fatty Liver, Weight Issues, SIBO & Autoimmune Disease.* Hay House; 2018.

[50] Johnson, Sonia. *The SisterWitch Conspiracy.* Createspace; 2010.

As women, I believe we need to stop feeling selfish when we prioritize self-care. Margo Anand wrote, "Loving yourself does not mean being self-absorbed or narcissistic, or disregarding others. Rather it means welcoming yourself as the most honored guest in your own heart, a guest worthy of respect, a lovable companion."[51] I would love to see more women honoring themselves in this way. Think of all the lengths we go to when we know we have a special guest coming. Why don't we reserve these efforts for ourselves? Why do we always save the best food and nicest atmosphere for everyone else?

Sara Sophia Eisenman has an entire book dedicated to hair[52]—something I admit I had not given much thought to since I stopped dying mine. I liked her approach so much I bought a copy for my besties at Christmas. Sara taught me that hair is an extension of our energy, vitality and Goddess-essence. All women, I believe, could do a better job of self-care. Sara's book took it to a whole new level—and is filled with at home, do-it-yourself suggestions that most of us can do inexpensively.

I have come to realize that many women don't feel all that great. I don't believe we can live well while constantly battling our own bodies. I think a large part of this comes with the defragmentation we endure under patriarchy. Susun Weed put it this way: "Most people think wholeness is body, mind, and spirit. But as soon as you say 'body, mind, and spirit,' you're no longer whole. You've just broken yourself up into pieces. What real wholeness is loving, accepting, and nourishing the parts of yourself that you find despicable."[53] Integrating all the different parts of our bodies and ourselves will bring us back to wholeness.

---

[51] Anand, Margo. *The Art of Sexual Ecstasy.* Jeremy P. Tarcher; *1988.*

[52] Eisenman, Sara Sophia. *Splendor: The Nazarite Method to Re(growing) Long, Strong, Healthy, Holy Hair.* Independently published; 2018.

[53] Beusman, Callie. "I Visited a Forest-Dwelling Witch to Cure My Crushing Existential Dread." *Broadly;* Dec 8, 2017.

Put Your Health First

This is a lesson you do not want to learn the hard way, but it seems like a lot of us need a knock on the head to prioritize our health.

Like everything else in this book, I recommend that you start where you're at. There are multiple chapters which cover specifics. Eating and sleeping well are critical. If you don't have energy or mental clarity, you can't change the world.

Capitalist Patriarchy relies on the unwaged labor of women. It depends on females to be too sick and tired to complain or do things differently. Audre Lorde wrote:

> "For to survive in the mouth of this dragon we call America, we have had to learn this first and most vital lesson—that we were never meant to survive. Not as human beings. And neither were most of you here today, Black or not. And that visibility which makes us most vulnerable is that which is also the source of our greatest strength. Because the machine will try to grind you into dust anyway, whether or not we speak. We can sit in our corners mute forever while our sisters and our selves are wasted, while our children are distorted and destroyed, while our earth is poisoned; we can sit in our safe corners mute as bottles, and we will still be no less afraid."[54]

Much to the dismay of my children's schools, I allow them to take mental health days—or to just stay home and rest when they need to. A few weeks ago, we were all feeling dreadfully tired, so I let everyone sleep in as long as they needed to. My daughter missed 3 days of school, but we also dodged the horrid 2-week flu that everyone else in her class caught.

---

[54] Lorde, Audre. "The Transformation of Silence into Language and Action." *Sister Outsider: Essays and Speeches*. Ten Speed Press; Reprint edition, 2007.

Teaching your children to listen to their bodies is invaluable wisdom—and something many of us were not taught ourselves. It is better to spend a day resting and avoid illness than to be knocked on your ass for 2 weeks because you refused to slow down. It took me a long time to learn this.

You probably have noted that I am not a huge fan of Western medicine. Unless there is an emergency, I would much rather listen to the wisdom of my own body and follow what works for me. Gabor Maté wrote that:

> "Settling for the view that illnesses, mental or physical, are primarily genetic allows us to avoid disturbing questions about the nature of the society in which we live. If 'science' enables us to ignore poverty or man-made toxins or a frenetic and stressful social culture as contributors to disease, we can look only to simple answers: pharmacological and biological."[55]

Until our dysfunctional world changes, I believe we should try to do everything we can to protect ourselves and our families. I am not a doctor, but I would like to provide some resources here that have been helpful to me. There are also quite a few book suggestions listed at the back of this book.

The book that helped me most initially is *You Can Heal Your Life* by Louise Hay. It is one of the handful of books I brought to Norway from Portland. I am still amazed at how spot-on her diagnoses are. As I was finishing this book, I developed hemorrhoids. *WTF?* I hadn't hemorrhoids since I was last pregnant 13 years ago. I opened the book and found that they were caused by a fear of deadlines.[56] I started laughing—and I felt like Louise was probably right there with me, laughing too. I had given myself a deadline on

---

[55] Maté, Gabor. *When the Body Says No: Understanding the Stress-Disease Connection*. Wiley; 2011.
[56] Hay, Louise. *You Can Heal Your Life*. Hay House; 1984.

this book that I knew I was not going to make. And it had literally come back to bite me in the butt.

I can't tell you how many times I listened to that book in my car during some of the worst years of my life. Her voice will stay with me always. Just knowing that I *could* heal, was so very comforting to me.

There is so much free health information online—and this is something to really take advantage of, particularly when health-care has become so costly in many places. I subscribe to a variety of naturopathic and functional medicine doctors. Probably the broadest variety of information can be found on Dr. Mercola's website, although as a woman, I always prefer to work with female doctors in person at this point.

Dr. Aviva Romm specializes in women's issues—and her work has been invaluable to me. I also love Dr. Kelly Brogan. And of course, Dr. Christiane Northrup is fantastic! You can also find great information via Dr. Axe, Dr. Mark Hyman and Hyla Cass MD. It can be difficult to keep up with all of these, so I generally just read what I can. It is also helpful to save up podcasts for days when you aren't feeling your best and need something inspiring to watch. Learn everything you can about your body—it is worth the time and investment!

No matter what your health challenges are, or how healthy you think you are, there is always something more you can do to make your body feel better. If you don't have your health, nothing else really matters. As Audre Lorde wrote, "Caring for myself is not self-indulgence, it is self-preservation, and that is an act of political warfare." We must begin to see it as such.

My Secret Weapon

I eat about a clove of garlic every day because it gives me an enormous amount of energy and wards off sickness. I learned this from my first husband, Hussein, who grew up eating a lot of garlic in Southern Lebanon. Many people think garlic gives you bad breath, and it can, but if you eat it regularly, your body adjusts to it. The Lebanese tend to mix it with parsley in salads and such, which also helps. Even if you do get bad breath when you eat garlic, I think you will find the benefits well worth it. And there is always gum!

I put a garlic clove in my vegetable juice, and another clove or two in my dinner salad. When I am feeling down on energy, I cut up several cloves during the course of the day and swallow them like vitamins with lemon-water. If I am sick, I will take as much as my stomach can tolerate. Garlic is an ingredient in just about every lunch and dinner I make. When I felt tired writing this book, I ate a clove of garlic—it works better than coffee! Drinking lots of lemon water along with it will also keep you hydrated and feeling well.

Garlic is amazing. It is a natural antibiotic and can assist with healing all manner of infections and viruses. Personally, I rarely take antibiotics from the pharmacy anymore—unless it is life-threatening. Garlic works without the side effects.[57]

Garlic is also an aphrodisiac,[58] and can be used to spice up your bedroom as well! Garlic also costs next to nothing, which is why it's a good place to start in terms of taking supplements.

Garlic is best fresh. You can grow your own garlic if you have space. Until I get my garden sorted out, I buy it in bulk at one of

---

[57] Levy, Jillian CHHC. "Are You at Risk for Antibiotic Resistance?" *Dr. Axe;* June 27, 2017.
[58] Barillaro, Maria and Jung, Alyssa RD. "Aphrodisiacs: What Are the Best Foods to Boost Your Sex Life?" *Readers Digest*; Jan 9, 2019.

the international markets here. It tends to be fresher than the local Norwegian supermarkets, as Norwegians aren't really known for eating spicy food.

If you can't do raw garlic, start cooking with it. Garlic is also delicious roasted. Just put an entire head or two on a cast iron pan, add a little olive oil, and roast it in the oven until it is brownish-black at the top. You can slide the garlic out easily once it is cool and add to toast or cracker. Best of all, garlic just tastes good!

Eat Well

What you eat effects everything else, so food is another top priority in my life. I put a lot of time and effort into most of our family meals. I share four children with my husband—and they can eat a lot. Food is one way I express my love for my family. Chopping lots of vegetables is also my daily stress release. It feels great after a long day!

Eat as many fresh fruits and vegetables as you can. Plant a garden. If you don't have a yard, join a community garden. My paternal grandparents both lived healthily until their nineties. They had an acre garden of just about everything you can think of. They ate seasonally and always had an abundance. The exercise is good for you too—and nothing tastes better than something you've just picked.

If you can juice, do it! I used to juice regularly but due to financial difficulties couldn't afford another juicer for many years after we moved to Norway. I purchased one as soon as I could and instantly felt a surge of energy. My favorite daily juice is a mixture of carrots, celery, sweet and spicy red peppers, cucumbers, cilantro, mint, garlic, ginger, and Brussel sprouts! I make one large pitcher in the morning and drink one glass first thing and another in the afternoon. I will share some recipes later in the book.

I also always have some sort of soup or broth going—and I aim for zero food waste in my home. So, for instance, when I juice, I set aside the head of the celery and add it to a broth later. Same with onion skins and any other shavings. Any leftovers can then be composted. You can also use things that most people toss out— like avocado seeds. I set mine aside and then grate them into my smoothies. There are some amazing health benefits from these seeds[59]—and it is oddly satisfying to grate the little balls!

---

[59] "10 surprising benefits of avocado seeds." *The Harald*; May 28, 2016.

One tidbit I will always remember from my paternal grandparents is the principal of sharing that both enabled them to get through the lean years while also creating some enjoyable memories. Because some things were rationed and food was limited, they hosted "sharing parties" where everyone would just bring whatever ingredients they happened to have. One of their favorite parties was a pancake party, where everyone stuffed themselves and danced into the evening.

There have been times in my life where I could barely afford a pack of spaghetti—so believe me, I know that it's not always easy to eat well. I remember my Nano telling me that there were years she ate almost nothing but potatoes. That always gets to me when I think about how generous she always was with everyone.

Whatever you have, bless it with love, and make the best meal you can. Your body needs and deserves your affection, and so do the ingredients that Mother Earth provides.

And, I hope this goes without saying in a feminist book, but please don't diet. You need food to function—and limiting yourself in this area will do nothing but make you tired and weak. As Naomi Wolf wrote years ago, "Dieting is the most potent political sedative in women's history; a quietly mad population is a tractable one."

If you stop eating processed junk foods, your body will tell you exactly what She needs—if you listen.

The female body is magical, stretching and retracting to a variety of sizes throughout our lifetimes—and to a lesser extent every single month! Rihanna once described this as having "the pleasure of a fluctuating body type." That's a refreshing outlook in a world where most females are taught to hate their bodies. I wish all women and girls could treasure themselves this way.

No one feels their best when they are hungry. And this goes for our community too. So, if you have a little extra—share with another sister. Even during my poorest days, I lived by this principal, and it always came back to me. There is always an extra plate of French fries or a bowl of soup that you can hand off to a neighbor. *Why not make their day?*

The feeling of abundance is also a habit that we form by not giving into fear and holding on too tightly. When we release this by sharing, we break the pattern that Capitalist Patriarchy has imposed on us. We are so much stronger together. We need all women, the world-over to be well-fed and well-nourished.

It is no accident that the highest proportion of those struggling with poverty and hunger are women. Malcom X said, "I'm not going to sit at your table and watch you eat, with nothing on my plate, and call myself a diner. Sitting at the table doesn't make you a diner, unless you eat some of what's on that plate." We need to have all women at the table—with a full plate of food.

Mother Earth provides for everyone. It is Capitalist Patriarchy that has stolen from Her bounty.

Don't Drink Too Much

The more I learn about the effects of alcohol on the body, the less appealing it is. I feel that it is also important to look at drinking from a critical (and feminist) perspective. A recent essay in *Quartz* often sparks anger from women when I post it to my Facebook page, but I think there is a lot of truth in what the author says as to why women drink.[60] Our lives are far less than ideal, and drinking can be a way of soothing that. Charlotte Davis Kasl's work goes into depth about this: "Patriarchy, hierarchy, and capitalism create, encourage, maintain, and perpetuate addiction and dependency. Patriarchy and hierarchy are based on domination and subordination, which result in fear. This fear is expressed by the dominators through control and violence, and in subordinated people through passivity and repression of anger. The external conflict of hierarchy between dominants and subordinates becomes internalized in individuals, creating personal inner chaos, anxiety and duality. To quell the inner conflict people resort to addictive substances and behavior."[61]

Women and men process alcohol differently, and it is not really in our own best interest to try to drink like 'one of the boys.' In Gabrielle Glaser's groundbreaking book about women and drinking, she wrote, "We consider alcohol a social equalizer, but we haven't been paying attention to the disparity of consequences."[62]

As Annie Grace noted in *This Naked Mind*,[63] the world has become one giant drinking advertisement, with leading roles in TV shows

---

[60] Coulter, Kristi. "Giving up alcohol opened my eyes to the infuriating truth about why women drink." *Quartz*; August 21, 2016.

[61] Davis Kasl, PhD, Charlotte. *Many Roads, One Journey: Moving Beyond the 12 Steps.* Harper Perennial; 1992.

[62] Glaser, Gabrielle. *Her Best-Kept Secret: Why Women Drink—And How They Can Regain Control.* Simon & Schuster; 2014.

[63] Grace, Annie. *This Naked Mind: Control Alcohol, Find Freedom, Discover Happiness & Change Your Life.* Avery; 2018.

and movies—and consumption at nearly all social events. *When did we start needing alcohol to enjoy everything?*

If you drink to suppress your emotions, you are also stripping yourself of some of your power. I often hear people say, "I need a drink." That is the worst time to take a drink. Your body is trying to tell you something in that moment—and if you take a drink instead of listening to what She wants or needs, you are missing a golden opportunity.

If you're a 'celebrate everything' kind of woman who likes red wine and the occasional beer—just drink in moderation.[64] Alcohol is expensive and too much of it is not good for our bodies.

A piece of advice I heard in a Reese Witherspoon movie once: *don't drink to feel better.* If you already feel bad, alcohol is not going to help. It will only make things fuzzier to deal with in the morning. Hangovers are the worst—and the ultimate expression of self-hatred. So, if you drink, don't overdo it. If you can't seem to drink without over-indulging, it may be time to consider stopping altogether. I believe in taking regular breaks from drinking and highly recommend Annie Grace's new book, *The Alcohol Experiment*—which will walk you through a 30-day break.

If you think you have a problem with alcohol[65] or other addictions, check out Patricia Lynn Reilly's *12 Steps from a Women's Perspective.* The amended steps are up on *The Girl God blog*. Note that Patricia's fourth step focuses on what *is* working: "Turning a merciful eye toward myself, I inventory both my life-affirming and

---

[64] Gabrielle Glaser notes in *Her Best-Kept Secret* that drinking recommendations vary by region of the world. Current U.S. Guidelines for women are no more than one drink per day. A recent UK study notes that there is no healthy level of alcohol consumption.
Boseley, Sarah. "No healthy level of alcohol consumption, says major study." The Guardian; 23 August 2018.

[65] See also, "Am I an Alcoholic?" by Laura McKowen.

ineffective habits of behaviors, and identify the habits of thought that inspire them."[66] I also recommend Charlotte Davis Kasl's *Women, Sex and Addiction*. Her systemic analysis of women, sex and all forms of addiction is eye-opening.

Many women who have been raped or abused understandably try to numb themselves. We must become more understanding of that struggle in ourselves as women—both individually and collectively. Gabor Maté wrote, "I don't have a single female patient in the Downtown Eastside of Vancouver who wasn't sexually abused... or abused, neglected and abandoned serially, over and over again."[67]

We need to let go of the stigma of addiction—something I will admit has been hard for me as someone whose life was severely hampered by an addict. Much of my recent reading has brought interesting contradictions to light for me. For example, when someone gives up smoking, they are congratulated. When someone gives up drinking, they are considered an alcoholic and stigmatized as someone who has a *problem.*

Both alcohol and cigarettes are highly addictive. We need to stop blaming people for becoming addicted to substances that are mass marketed and consumed to our detriment. The only people who win at this game are the alcohol and cigarette companies.

We also must begin to strive for lives in which numbing ourselves is no longer necessary.

---

[66] Reilly, Patricia Lynn. *A Deeper Wisdom: The 12 Steps from a Woman's Perspective.* http://www.patricialynnreilly.com/mq-e-books.html

[67] Maté, Gabor. *In the Realm of Hungry Ghosts: Close Encounters with Addiction.* North Atlantic Books; 2010.

Skip Church

If you have read my previous books, this bit may be distressing for you. But as I have moved further on my journey, I no longer believe that going to church—or attending the services of any patriarchal religion is good for women, at all. As Barbara G. Walker wrote, "Women who cling to the biblical world-view will never achieve their full humanity."[68] You can't nurture your self-esteem and well-being while attending an institution that regularly devalues women and girls.

I used to believe the progressive churches were better. But as I healed my life, I could no longer stomach those either. The last time I attended the progressive church I once adored, I was cringing the entire time.

I still love the people who attend my old church—and I certainly don't blame anyone for going to church, mosque or synagogue. I went to 2 out of 3 for most of my life! But I can't endorse any of them anymore. As Monica Sjöö and Barbara Mor wrote decades ago:

> "We need a new, global spirituality—an organic spirituality that belongs innately to all of us, as the children of earth. A genuine spirituality that utterly refutes the moralistic, manipulative patriarchal systems, the mechanistic religions that seek to divide us—that control and oppress us by successfully dividing us. We need a spirituality that acknowledges our earthly roots as evolutionary and sexual beings, just as we need an ontology that acknowledges earth as a conscious and spiritual being. We need this organic, global spirituality because we are ready to evolve as a globally conscious species. We are at the point where we must evolve or die."[69]

---

[68] Walker, Barbara. *Man Made God*. Stellar House Publishing; 2010.
[69] Sjöö, Monica and Mor, Barbara. *The Great Cosmic Mother: Rediscovering*

Our systematic economic suppression underlies all other oppressions. We must begin to take an honest *closer look* at how religion and money work together to subjugate women. Sister Joan Chittister wrote:

> "Women have been locked out of full humanity and full participation in religious institutions and society at large. This marginalization of women masquerades as 'protecting' them and even 'exalting' them. Instead, these attitudes serve to deny the human race the fullness of female gifts and a female perspective on life. As a result, women make up two-thirds of the hungry of this world. And women are two-thirds of the illiterate of this world. And women are two-thirds of the poorest of the poor, because they lack access to the resources and recognition men take for granted. That's not an accident. That is a policy—one supported by religious institutions that call such discrimination 'women's place' and 'God's will.'"

If quitting church doesn't work for you, no worries. That's just where I am at now.[70] At the very least, you might reconsider directing your tithe to a more woman-friendly organization or charity.[71]

---

the Religion of the Earth. HarperOne; 2nd edition, 1987.

[70] I fully understand the power of community that many people feel from their religious communities is also immensely important, and I will touch on that in another chapter.

[71] See a longer discussion on this in my essay, "Money and the Elephant in the Room," which is also available on my blog.
Hendren, Trista. "Money and the Elephant in the Room." *Whatever Works: Feminists of Faith Speak*. A Girl God Anthology; 2015.

Celebrate Everything!

Life shouldn't be a drudgery. Yes, patriarchy sucks, and there are a million ways it screws us over—but there is so much more to life!

Enjoy every single thing you can. Celebrate even the smallest accomplishments! Eat cake! Take a long, leisurely walk! Make love! Sing your favorite song as loud as you want to! Belly-laugh! Pick a bouquet of flowers! Savor a long bath! Sue Patton Thoelle wrote: "We are daughters of life's generosity, constantly surrounded by the altruism of Mother Earth and the myriad blessings present in work and relationships. It is our birthright to joyously claim this bountiful inheritance."[72]

I believe the feeling of scarcity enforced on females robs us of more than just what it would seem on the surface. Joy seems almost gluttonous when you are a grown woman—especially if you have children.

I try to celebrate at least one thing every day. On the days that I just can't, I indulge myself by reading as much as I want or watching a funny show. We must begin to remember old ways of being, even if just by reading inspirational books. Robin Wall Kimmerer wrote this glorious passage:

> "The depths of the Feminine, languorous in the sun, embraced by beautiful connective tissue that is this moss: I want to stand by the river in my finest dress. I want to sing, strong and hard, and stomp my feet with a hundred others so that the waters hum with our happiness. I want to dance for the renewal of the world."[73]

---

[72] Thoelle, Sue Patton. *The Woman's Book of Soul: Meditations for Courage, Confidence & Spirit.* Conari Press; New Ed edition, 2000.

[73] Wall Kimmerer, Robin. *Braiding. Sweetgrass: Indigenous Wisdom, Scientific Knowledge and the Teachings of Plants.* Milkweed Editions; 2013.

There is something really deep in what she said. *Did you catch it?*

"I want to dance for the renewal of the world."

There is something about women dancing—really dancing, for *themselves*—that diminishes patriarchy. Same goes for laughing. My sister and I used to go into hysterics at the dinner table and it would drive my father insane. We literally could not contain ourselves, despite his best efforts to make us stop and be proper.

Mary Daly touched on this in *Gyn/Ecology:*

> "There is nothing like the sound of women really laughing! The roaring laughter of women is like the roaring of the eternal sea. Hags can cackle and roar at themselves, but more and more, one hears them roaring at the reversal that is patriarchy... this laughter is the one true hope, for as long as it is audible, there is evidence that someone is seeing through the Dirty Joke."[74]

When was the last time you had a good belly-laugh? When is the last time you danced your heart out? Don't discount joy—it is our birthright after all! Terry Tempest Williams reminds us, "Once upon a time, when women were birds, there was the simple understanding that to sing at dawn and to sing at dusk was to heal the world through joy. The birds still remember what we have forgotten, that the world is meant to be celebrated."[75]

---

[74] Daly, Mary. *Gyn/Ecology: The Metaethics of Radical Feminism*. Beacon Press; 1990.

[75] Tempest Williams, Terry. *When Women Were Birds: Fifty-four Variations on Voice*. Sarah Crichton Books; 2012.

Get to Know your Neighbors

I grew up on a very quirky street, and I can still remember most of my neighbors quite vividly as they were all eccentric. We had a lady with purple hair who walked her cat on a leash, a horny Danish plumber—and loads of other characters. But we also had a strong sense of community. My dad put in a porch swing on the front porch and have fond memories of sitting there watching my neighbors—or playing with the other kids in the little play house he built for us. Nearly everyone has moved or died now, but our wonderful Jewish neighbors across the street are still there holding down the fort—and this gives me great comfort.

I have lived on many different streets and had many kinds of neighbors. I have an intense memory from living in the suburbs and watching my neighbor's house burn down one night. It struck me that they lived right across the street and I had never even met them! At that point in my life, I lived in a neighborhood where everyone had gardeners and none of my neighbors really interacted with each other. *What a shame!* It was such an odd feeling being out on the street with people I lived close to but had never met. I remember thinking that I should invite them to stay with us—and then not offering because we had never even talked before.

Our last home in Portland was a wonderful spot for us. We had awesome neighbors across the street with a handy husband and a mom who also home-schooled. We were able to share field trips and experiences with our girls. And then girls could also entertain themselves for hours (without TV)—which helped us both out. Our neighbor also had a gorgeous garden, and she often shared. I don't think she will ever know how much this helped me with my own health! She grew the best monster kale—and I would make amazing salads for close to nothing. We also had a wonderful bench on the front porch, so neighbors would often stop by in the evening to chat for a bit.

When we moved into our current house in Bergen, the neighbors were quick to offer to share tools. Our next-door neighbor on one side noticed that we did not have a lawn mower and offered to share theirs. We noticed that they did not have a power washer, and offered to share ours. This is so much more economical than each person going out to purchase everything they need. The man on the other side has just about every single thing you can think of tool-wise, so my daughter shares her fresh baked cookies with him.

In the last decades, we have lost the sense of community that neighborhoods used to provide. Bringing back community-focused living will take some effort, but it will be worth it.

Join a Local Red Tent or Women's Circle

Men have been making decisions for and about women for centuries behind closed doors. Men have decided largely which scriptures should be used, which laws should be passed, and what our reproductive choices should be. Men's decisions about what is and isn't important have led us to war and the destruction of Mother Earth.

It is critically important that women meet in their own circles to determine their own realities. There is no substitute for meeting face-to-face. Gloria Steinem recently said in an interview, "If I had to name the most important discovery of my life, it would be the portable community of talking circles; groups that gather with all five senses and allow consciousness to change."

My friend Karen Lee Moon has even designed an app specifically to help women find their own circle.[76] If you don't find a community you like locally, consider creating your own. It is hard to understand the power of a women's circle until you have been a part of one. This is magical, sacred time. It doesn't have to be fancy or well-planned. In fact, sometimes the simpler the better.

A simple circle of women where you all introduce yourself via your mother-line is a wonderful starting place. Go back as far as you can remember.

> *I am Trista Lee, Daughter of Patricia Lee, Granddaughter of Betty JoAnne, Great Granddaughter of Betty Maurine...*

This always leaves me very emotional, both in remembering my own mother-line and in hearing other women recite back theirs. Women are often not recognized in our world—so the simple act of doing so is extraordinarily healing. HeatherAsh Amara reminds us: "For thousands of years, in tribes and villages around the

---

[76] You can find the Divine Feminine App at www.TheDFApp.com

world women have come together in circles to share, to teach, to listen, to learn. The pulse of these women still beats within us. Their wisdom flows through time, whispering to us the song of female connection and beauty. We only need to stop long enough and put our ear to our heart to hear the call."[77]

The important thing is to show up—and see what happens. Women coming together in circles is always amazing. As Jeanette LeBlanc wrote, "A circle of women may just be the most powerful force known to humanity. If you have one, embrace it. If you need one, seek it. If you find one, for the love of all that is good and holy, dive in. Hold on. Love it up. Get Naked. Let them see you. Let them hold you. Let your reluctant tears fall. Let yourself rise fierce and love gentle. You will be changed. The very fabric of your being will be altered by this, if you allow it. Please, please allow it."[78]

---

[77] Amara. HeatherAsh. *Warrior Goddess Training: Become the Woman You Are Meant to Be*. Hierophant Publishing; 2014.
[78] Jeanette has a fabulous piece of art with this quote on her Etsy page.

Honor Your Moon Cycle

If we are ever to reverse patriarchal thought, we must reach to the roots of our oppressions. The brilliance of patriarchy is that it is so subliminal and insidious. Until reading Helen Hwang's *Mago Almanac*, I had never given much thought to the patriarchal calendar—even though I produced one for 5 years—aside from my growing annoyance of trying to incorporate the moon phases into a more "traditional" calendar. I came to realize the idiocy of trying to incorporate liberation for women into a completely patriarchal idea. For this reason, I stopped producing my Girl God calendar a few years ago.

Our calendars shape our days and our very lives. As Helen Hye-Sook Hwang explains, "Debunking a patriarchal calendar for what it does is the key to disempowering patriarchy as a whole... The 12-month calendar is a patriarchal invention intended to replace the earlier 13-month sidereal calendar... The 29.5 day lunar calendar has prevented us from seeing what the moon actually does... In order to disconnect the moon cycle and women's fertility cycle, patriarchal calendars removed the 13th month and made 12 months in a year."[79]

Let us begin the process of weeding out every single thing that blinds us to our power and path to liberation—including men's clocks, calendars and timelines.

I would suggest also adding some seasonal ceremonies into your life as well. If you are new to these celebrations, I would strongly suggest Glenys Livingstone's *PaGaian Cosmology Meditations* CD collection which supports the preparation and performing of ritual for each Seasonal celebration, including the Solstices and Equinoxes and the cross-quarter days of Early Spring/Imbolc, Beltaine/High Spring, Lammas/Late Summer, and Samhain/Deep

---

[79] Hwang, Helen Hye-Sook. *Mago Almanac: 13 Month 28 Day Calendar.* Mago Books; 2018.

Autumn. Personally, I still celebrate ALL holidays, but adding these in has been a rich addition to my life.

For at least a decade, my favorite women's studies and writing professor from college has sent me a moon phases calendar. I keep this up on the wall for the entire family to see—and track my cycle via the phases of the moon.[80]

If you menstruate, I recommend getting to know your cycle as well as the moon phases to understand the needs of your body.[81] Learn how to best utilize your creative times while honoring your down periods. As Dr. Christiane Northrup explains:

> "The menstrual cycle governs the flow not only of fluids but of information and creativity. We receive and process information differently at different times in our cycles. I like to describe menstrual cycle wisdom this way: From the onset of menstruation until ovulation, we're ripening an egg and—symbolically, at least—preparing to give birth to someone (or something) else, a role that society honors.
>
> Premenstrually, the "veil" between the worlds of the seen and unseen, the conscious and the unconscious, is much thinner. We have access to parts of our often unconscious selves that are less available to us at all other times of the month. In fact, it has been shown experimentally that the right hemisphere of the brain—the part associated with intuitive knowing—becomes more active premenstrually, while the left hemisphere becomes less active."[82]

Personally, I try to take a day off on the first day of my period. If this is not possible for you, at least try to be as easy on yourself as

---

[80] You can order one of these at www.snakeandsnake.com.
[81] Another important resource is www.sisterzeus.com.
[82] Northrup, Christiane M.D. "Wisdom of the Menstrual Cycle: Honoring the Sacred Moon Cycle." www.drnorthrup.com February 26, 2007.

possible and rest during the evening. This is a day that someone else can cook and pamper you. Inga Muscio wrote, "It takes a lot of time, focus and energy to realize the enormity of being the ocean with your very own tide every month. However, by honoring the demands of bleeding, our blood gives something in return. The crazed bitch from irritation hell recedes. In her place arises a side of ourselves with whom we may not—at first—be comfortable. She is a vulnerable, highly perceptive genius who can ponder a given issue and take her world by storm. When we're quiet and bleeding, we stumble upon the solutions to dilemmas that've been bugging us all month. Inspiration hits and moments of epiphany rumba 'across de tundra of our senses. In this mode of existence one does not feel antipathy towards a bodily ritual so profoundly and routinely reinforces our cuntpower."[83]

I often find solutions for things during these quiet moments and have come to value my bleeding time enormously. As Tamara Slayton explained:

> "We have lost years of educating ourselves to the mysteries of ovulation, menstruation, conception and menopause as we gave over the "research" to others... the process by which women make themselves susceptible to manipulation by a science without soul begins at first menstruation. Women lose a significant aspect of who they are when they deny the demands and rewards of the female body. Ultimately alienation from your own physical experience leads to manipulation by those who do know the value of ovum and lining."[84]

Honor your blood. It is sacred—not dirty. Most commercial sanitary products are not good for the environment or your

[83] Muscio, Inga. *Cunt: A Declaration of Independence.* Seal Press; 2002.

[84] Slayton, Tamara. *Reclaiming the Menstrual Matrix: Evolving Feminine Wisdom.* Lantern Books; 2002.

vulva.[85] I used to love my cups, but now I don't even want to touch plastic, let alone put it inside me. You can buy wonderful reusable cotton pads on Etsy. I bought a 6-pack years ago and they are still like new. Save your blood and give it back to Mother Earth. It is wonderfully nurturing. I pour mine on the soil of my indoor plants and herbs as well.

If you are menopausal, I bow to your crone wisdom. I can't (and shouldn't) offer much advice (yet) but the two books I have heard recommended again and again are *The Wisdom of Menopause: Creating Physical and Emotional Health During the Change* by Christiane Northrup M.D. and *New Menopausal Years: Alternative Approaches for Women 30-90* by Susun S. Weed. Those are the books I will start with personally.

Wherever you are in your life, it is important to honor it. As Jean Shinoda Bolen wrote:

> "Women's mysteries, the blood mysteries of the body, are not the same as the physical realities of menstruation, lactation, pregnancy, and menopause; for physiology to become mystery, a mystical affiliation must be made between a woman and the archetypal feminine. A woman must sense, know or imagine herself as Woman, as Goddess, as an embodiment of the feminine principle… Under patriarchy this connection has been suppressed; there are no words or rituals that celebrate the connection between a woman's physiological initiations and spiritual meaning."[86]

Returning to our Divine connection regularly removes the splintering effects of patriarchy.

---

[85] "Plastic periods: menstrual products and plastic pollution." *Friends of the Earth*; October 15, 2018.

[86] Bolen, Jean Shinoda M.D. *Goddesses in Older Women: Archetypes in Women over Fifty*. Harper; 2014.

Stop Apologizing for your Existence

Many of us grew up apologizing for things that are not our fault to keep the peace. As Patricia Lynn Reilly noted:

> "Women are much more experienced at using the words 'I'm sorry' than men are. These words are not a mere perfunctory bow to politeness when uttered by most women. They contain a self-depreciating quality as if we are apologizing for our very existence—as if the answer to 'what's wrong with me' is embedded within our femaleness. The search for an answer to the question 'What's wrong with me' consumes our valuable time, depletes our precious life energy, exhausts our limited resources, and distracts from taking responsibility for our lives."[87]

It took me a long time to realize that I had nothing to be sorry for. Growing up as a girl in the church taught me that I needed to be on my knees every night, begging for forgiveness. On Sundays, there was usually an altar call, where I would often make a public display of just how 'bad' I was. This set up a horrible precedent. When females are taught to be contrite, they learn not to fight. I am pretty damned certain none of the males in the church— including those who abused me—are sorry for anything. Females who feel ashamed are easier to control. SARK advised,

> "Stop apologizing and saying, 'I'm sorry' so much. Women have a terrible habit of apologizing for everything (even their own existence.) One time, I bumped into a woman— hard—and she said automatically, 'I'm sorry.' I had bumped into her! Sorry in the Dictionary says this: wretches,

---

[87] Reilly, Patricia Lynn. *Be Full of Yourself!: The Journey from Self-Criticism to Self-Celebration.* Open Window Creations; 1998.

miserable, inferior in worth or quality. We are not this! We have a right to live wild, succulent lives."[88]

Be mindful of the words you use and how you talk about yourself (and to yourself). Catch yourself before apologizing unnecessarily. If you mess up, by all means, say you are sorry. But never apologize for your glorious female self.

Females are taught they are 'wrong' from birth for not being male. Everything in our world is set up for the benefit of men. It is time for us to reclaim a world of our own. If you struggle with this, here's a mantra that I love from Patricia Lynn Reilly:

> "My thoughts are my own—I will not modify them to receive the approval of others. My feelings are my own—I will not silence them to make others comfortable. My life is my own—I will not shape it according to the expectations of others. I live in harmony with my natural cycles, deepest wisdom, and truest self. And so it is."[89]

---

[88] SARK. *Succulent Wild Woman: Dancing with your Wonder-full Self!* Simon Schuster; 1997.
[89] Reilly, Patricia Lynn. *Be Full of Yourself!: The Journey from Self-Criticism to Self-Celebration.* Open Window Creations; 1998.

Learn to be Direct

Most girls are taught under patriarchy to submit to male authority to some extent. Having raised male and female children, I can tell you this is still true.

I am actively working with my 12-year-old daughter to ask directly for what she wants. Even being raised mostly under my feminist framework, I find this is often difficult for her. (Not so for my son or stepsons.)

When I see my daughter waffling, I stop her and ask her to pause. *What do you really want right now?* Ask for that.

Whenever possible, I try to give her what she asks for to establish a positive identification with being direct.

Many women become passive-aggressive because they resent being forced into passivity—and aggression (or even assertiveness) is not acceptable for females. So, changing this mindset is not easy—especially if you have spent your entire life following this pattern.

Start small. *What do you want for dinner? How do you want to spend your evening?* State your desires and see how it feels. Unless your partner is totally self-absorbed, s/he will appreciate it when you assert yourself. At times, I have felt 'too bitchy' with my husband, who I am very direct with. He assures me that he loves it —because, he never has to guess with me. He knows where he stands at all times and that I am there—present, in the moment, and doing something I actually want to do.

Learn how to say no. Oftentimes this takes practice and trial and error for women. If you find yourself committing to do something that you really don't want to do, stop and pause for a minute. Ask yourself *why* you are doing it—and give yourself more time to make a decision. And, remember—you always have the right to change your mind. You can go back and tell the other person that you are learning how to take better care of yourself and made the wrong decision in haste.

This can also be done in the workplace. When I was a mortgage broker, we had mandatory weekly meetings that I dreaded. Every week I dutifully attended the meeting and complained about it later. I finally realized that the meetings were unproductive and a waste of my time—which was limited as a single mother with two young children. So, I told my boss I would not go anymore. He wanted to keep me employed with his company, so he agreed I could skip them. No one else could believe I got out of attending, and would ask in amazement, *how did you do that?*

I just asked.

If you don't ask, you don't get.

The answer may not always be the one you want, but you have nothing to lose by trying.

When we begin to recognize our worth, we also realize that people are often willing to meet our needs when we are direct about them.

Don't Settle in Love

This may seem like a repeat of an earlier chapter, but I intentionally put it in here twice because it pains me to see so many women in less than adequate relationships.

It is possible to have a loving and peaceful relationship. When there is constant arguing and drama, it is a sign that the relationship is not right.

It is possible to have a disagreement and handle it peacefully and lovingly. It is possible to be completely wide-open with someone and not have him use it against you later.

These things may seem obvious, but they were totally out of my radar when I was married to my children's father. Our relationship was so off-balance and dysfunctional that I completely lost my grounding. The only really strong example of love I witnessed was that of my paternal grandparents who were happily married for more than 64 years. If I hadn't had that example, I don't think I would have found my way back to a good relationship. They were my guiding stars and I believe they sent me an angel in the form of the man I am with now.

Sometimes it takes a few relationships that *don't* work to realize what you *do* want.

When I was completing my certification process with *Imagine a Woman*, there was an entire segment on relationships, that I now offer on my website. I think it was one of the best things I have ever seen on relationships. It was such a moment of clarity for me, and it was so simple—just noticing how you *feel* in someone's presence.

> "After each encounter with a new friend or potential lover, ask yourself:

"How did I feel in his/her presence?"
Underline or highlight the words that best describe your
feelings. "I felt _____ in his/her presence today."

excited
turned on
challenged
opened
energized
---
fearful
restrained
cautious
on guard
misunderstood[90]

For the first time in my life, I feel only what is in the top section. And this has been my daily experience for the past 8 years.

Sometimes, as women, I think it's very difficult for us to give up even a very bad relationship. It is ingrained in us from childhood that a relationship is the primary thing that gives us value. When we realign with our feelings, we know what is right for us when it comes. We can also be happy and perfectly content on our own, without a relationship.

---

[90] Reilly, Patricia Lynn. "Relationships from the Inside Out." Imagine a Woman International, 2010. Available on my website.

Learn Some Witchcraft

There is a reason why women are afraid to be witches. Silvia Federici discusses some of the reasons behind the witch-hunts and their tie to the rise of capitalism in her recent book, *Witches, Witch-Hunting, and Women:*

> "Women were those most likely to be victimized because they were the most 'disempowered' by these changes, especially older women, who often rebelled against their impoverishment and social exclusion and who constituted the bulk of the accused. In other words, women were charged with witchcraft because the restructuring of rural Europe at the dawn of capitalism destroyed their means of livelihood and the basis of their social power, leaving them with no resort but dependence on the charity of the better-off at a time when communal bonds were disintegrating and a new morality was taking hold that criminalized begging and looked down upon charity, the reputed path to eternal salvation in the medieval world."[91]

Maybe you identify as a witch, and maybe you don't—but learning a few spells can be empowering. Z Budapest's *The Holy Book of Women's Mysteries* is a great place to start. If you are feeling hopeless about your rape or other sexual abuse, you can learn how to hex your rapist. As Z says, *if you can't hex, you can't heal.* Witchcraft is not evil—I see it as restorative justice.

There still remain many misconceptions and fear around witchcraft and many females are taught to doubt and suppress their power from birth for this very reason. This is what being a witch means to me: "Witches cast spells, not to do evil, but to promote changes of consciousness. Witches cast spells as acts of redefinition. To respell the world means to redefine the root of

---

[91] Federici, Silvia. *Witches, Witch-Hunting, and Women.* PM Press; 2018.

our being. It means to redefine us and therefore change us by returning us to our original consciousness of magical-evolutionary processes. This consciousness is within us, in our biology and in our dreams. It works on subliminal levels, whether or not we are aware of it, because it is the energy of life and imagination. When we are aware of it, it works for us, as the energy of destiny. And it is powerful, with the genuine power of biological life and cosmic imagination."[92]

Witchcraft does not have to be a fancy spell with candles and all the fixings. Witchcraft can be as simple as making an intention. I like to keep a journal to see how many dreams I can bring into existence just by writing them down and reviewing them occasionally.

---

[92] Sjöö, Monica and Mor, Barbara. *The Great Cosmic Mother: Rediscovering the Religion of the Earth*. HarperOne; 2nd edition, 1987.

Consider Scandinavia

You might think this is my most outlandish idea yet, but I don't say this lightly. I moved to Norway nearly 4 years ago as someone who had lived in relative poverty, without child support, without speaking the language, without a "real" job and without any money in the bank. *How?* I decided that I would. I didn't know how I would do it when I made my resolution, but I knew that I would, someday. (And no, my husband is not wealthy—he works far below his pay grade at a non-profit environmental organization —he's an idealist like me!)

I was worn out from life and wanted to live with Anders, who I had been in a long-distance relationship with for over 4 years. This had taken a toll on both of our finances, and there was no slush fund for anything.

I sold almost everything I had, but I still did not have enough money for our tickets. I stayed with close friends with my children until we had the funds together. It was the worst flight possible— more than 28 hours—but we made it here and I have no regrets.

My point is, where there is a will, there is often a way. The way I did things is probably not appealing to most people—we lived in a 800-square-foot flat with 2-4 children (depending on custody arrangements) for 2 years and don't own a car. I had to be really creative with our food budget and we had zero 'fun' money. But, life is ruled by your priorities, and often requires some sacrifices to get the things you *really* want.

More importantly, living abroad has allowed me to imagine other ways of being. Patricia Lynn Reilly wrote that, "Until we imagine something, it remains an impossibility. Once imagined, it becomes our experience." I believe those living in countries where people are not taken care of should begin to imagine and dream up new ways of life. Norway was not always a great place to live. It took time, dedication—and yes, *dreams*.

I always say that Norway is not perfect, but it is about as good as it gets for women and children. I will continue to imagine a world that provides for women and children everywhere.

I love living in Norway because everyone is taken care of here. When we left Portland, we literally had to step around people sleeping on the street to get my daughter to school. This was heartbreaking to see every day. I am proud to live in a city where I have never seen a homeless person. Certainly, homelessness still remains the world over, but living here has taught me that this need not be the case. It is my firm belief that there is more than enough in this world for everybody.

We also have free medical care here. For everyone. Children have free dental care. Both my children have braces at the moment, and the government paid for about half of that expense too. 18 months after moving here, I spent a week in the hospital. I left without paying a cent for my stay. My only cost was about $35 for my prescriptions when I left. I have friends in the United States who had to file for bankruptcy after spending a week in the hospital.

The saddest thing for me as an American is to see so many people struggling needlessly. If the U.S. didn't waste money on endless wars that destroy other countries, there would be ample funds to take care of each and every person.

Until enough people stand up and say NO MORE, it will continue to happen. Until then, we all must do our very best to take better care of each other.

A move across the globe is not practical for most people—but looking elsewhere can be invaluable in terms of instigating change. Let us envision and create the countries that we *want* to live in—and demand the changes that would bring them into existence.

Invest in Yourself

I have watched a lot of women spend hundreds of dollars on a pair of jeans or makeup to look better for a certain guy—but then hesitate to spend money on something that would actually make their lives better.

Needless to say, this frustrates me immensely.

Even if you don't have a dime to spend on anything, your time and energy are also assets. When women stop giving so much of themselves away to men, they will have more time, energy and money to spend on themselves. Daphne Rose Kingma wrote that, "Everything worth having costs something, and the price of true love is self-knowledge. Becoming acquainted with yourself is a price well worth paying."

Some of us are not even aware of how we spend our time and our money, which is why I think calendars and budgeting are important. Make sure to schedule time for yourself into your calendar too—and time to be with other women.

We can reinvest how we spend our time. Instead of doing laundry, cooking and cleaning house for the men in our lives, we can support single mothers and elderly women in our communities. Don't you worry—I guarantee you there is not an able-bodied man alive who can't figure out how to do these things himself, especially when it involves food. Moses Seenarine wrote that: "Women are responsible for household food preparation in 85-90 percent in a wide range of countries. Neoliberal cyborg capitalism is profitable only due to their exploitation of unpaid female labor in household production and in their reproduction of workers. Unpaid care work would constitute between 10 and 50 per cent of GDP if it was assigned a monetary value."[93]

---

[93] Seenarine, Moses. *Cyborgs Versus the Earth Goddess: Men's Domestication of*

I love my husband and my son, but they both do their own laundry, dishes and vacuuming. I expect them to do their fair share around the house—without being asked. That is what living in a community—as a family—means.

We have subverted the idea of family to where the wife/mother/women/daughters do all the work in the home—and the men control all the money from their higher paid employment.

Females are bred to be slaves around the world—both at home and in our so-called paid positions. It can be rewarding to be a caregiver, but there are tremendous costs to consider that will likely never be recouped. I cared for 3 of my grandparents while they were dying. I wouldn't trade that for anything. That said, when my money ran out and I needed help, there was little to be found.

The same goes for taking care of children. I will likely never recover from my years as a single mother. And not only does the pay gap widen with each child you have, you also have significantly less available in retirement, where women are also extremely vulnerable.[94]

Contrary to what they told us, women cannot *have it all*. Life is quite often not for the faint of heart. It requires tough choices and sacrifices. You must actively decide how you want to spend your time and money going forward. Whatever time you invest now in deciding what sort of life you want will pay off ten-fold later. The investments you make in yourself will change the entire world.

Women and Animals and Female Resistance. Xpyr Pres; 2017.

[94] Miller, Claire Cain. "The 10-Year Baby Window That Is the Key to the Women's Pay Gap." *The New York Times;* April 9, 2018.

Support Other Women

We will always be considered inferior to men if we don't bind together and re-discover our power. Since we are behind in nearly every way economically, we must carefully consider the money we do have—and use it to support each other whenever possible.

Terry Tempest Williams wrote that, "The sin we commit against each other as women is lack of support."[95] It is critically important that we support each other spiritually, emotionally and economically. Just the simple task of buying a feminist book penned by a woman—or a piece of artwork created by a female—is an investment in yourself, your children and your grandchildren. It also supports a project that empowers other women and enables the dreamer to continue her work.

It also gives women more ability to break away from the systems that support the gender pay gap. When women open their own businesses, they have more flexibility and opportunities for growth and income.

I believe women must radically reconsider every single dollar they spend. The fact is that woman-owned businesses, writers and artists need money to survive. We have to reallocate the limited funds we have as women if we truly want to see changes in women's lives globally.

This is what it comes down to for me whenever I think about making a purchase: *who is benefiting?* Will this item or service make my life better—or my children's lives easier—now or in the near future? Am I supporting a person or business that is in alignment with my values? Will this purchase destroy Mother Earth or harm Her inhabitants?

---

[95] Tempest Williams, Terry. *When Women Were Birds: Fifty-four Variations on Voice*. Sarah Crichton Books; 2012.

I don't have all the answers. I still have not found a way around Amazon or a woman-centered approach to Facebook. Both solutions need to be found as soon as possible. I would also love to see a global emergency fund put into place for women. We can all help each other when the inevitable emergency pops up. I can't think of a single woman I have ever known who has not been stuck at some point in her life.

We must also ensure that no woman, anywhere in the world, enters her crone years in poverty. The crone should be relaxing and reflecting on her glorious life—not slaving away at McDonalds or living in her car. When we accept that a crone should live like this, we also lose her immense wisdom.

We cannot accomplish any of our goals for liberation if we do not understand how money functions[96]—and most importantly, if we don't work together. Our individualistic lives are killing us. We need to work together and fight back—hard. We can't change everything today, but we can find creative solutions to make our individual and collective lives easier. We can live communally, share resources and refuse to spend one-penny on anything that does not empower us as females.

Until we have economic equality, I urge you to consider how you spend your money—and do it in a way that honors yourself, Mother Earth and your sisters around the globe.

For example, if you go out to eat, patronize a woman-owned restaurant. When you need a gift, search on Etsy first. Begin to prioritize books, CDs and art created by women. Every-single-place we spend our money has the potential to change our world. As Kathleen Dean Moore said, "Deciding we won't drive to that chain grocery store and buy that imported pineapple is a path of liberation. Deciding to walk to the farmers' market and buy those

---

[96] See also, "Sri Sraddhalu Ranade on Money: How it works and why it doesn't" on Youtube.

fresh, local peas is like spitting in the eye of the industries that would control us. Every act of refusal is also an act of assent. Every time we say no to consumer culture, we say yes to something more beautiful and sustaining. Life is not something that we go through or what happens to us; it's something we create by our decisions. We can drift through our lives, or we can use our time, our money and our strength to model behaviors we believe in, to say, "This is who I am."[97]

Even if you are limited financially, you can still support other women by sharing their work on social media. A few other ideas:

- Ask your local library to carry books by independent publishers and self-published women authors.
- Go to museum and art exhibits by women. Buy their art whenever possible.
- Offer to baby-sit for a new or single mother.

I spent years not being able to do anything social. When you are truly broke, there is no funding for a social life. If it were not for my mother, I would never had done anything fun for many, many years. It can be painful to be left out in this way, so if you see a sister who seems to be struggling, you might offer to help. If you have money to attend an event comfortably, pay another woman's way as well.

We can refuse to participate in our own economic subordination. If we work collectively, we can also reallocate money and other resources in a way that works for everyone.

---

[97] Democker, Mary. "If Your House Is On Fire: Kathleen Dean Moore On The Moral Urgency Of Climate Change." *The Sun;* December 2012.

When You Give... Be Intentional

I used to work for a couple that were about the happiest people I've ever met. I attribute this to their generosity. Their favorite expression was, "You can't out-give the universe!"

Many of us are privileged in some way. There is almost always something you can share—even if it's just a hug or some of your time.

I have stopped giving to religious and 'humanitarian' organizations for the most part. I prefer to give directly to women who need help. I know some people hesitate to do so without the tax write off, but I feel better knowing that my money is being utilized 100% by someone who truly needs and appreciates it.[98]

Don't be stingy, but do evaluate whether you are giving too much. Life should be give and take. So many of us give ourselves away. I believe that when we shift our giving to include primarily women and children, this dynamic will change drastically.

---

[98] See a longer discussion on this in my essay, "Money and the Elephant in the Room," which is also available on my blog.
Hendren, Trista. "Money and the Elephant in the Room." *Whatever Works: Feminists of Faith Speak*. A Girl God Anthology, 2015.

Keep a Journal

I keep a dream journal next to my bed and try to write down what I remember upon waking.

Your dreams often provide insight into which direction to go with your life or may help you decipher things that don't make sense to you. My grandparents and other wise wo/men often appear to me in my dreams to give direction. Keeping a journal helps you keep track of patterns that you might miss otherwise.

My maternal grandmother came to me in a dream shortly before I finished writing this book. I had been stuck on a few points, and she gave me the answers I needed to move forward. At the very end, my paternal grandmother came to me—just to give me a big hug. I treasure my dreams and the loved ones who come to visit me long after they have left this earthly realm.

As an avid reader, I also include notes on my favorite books. Writing down quotes helps me to remember the important things I learned—and implement them.

I also keep a goal journal where I write down everything I want to happen or have. It works. Nearly everything gets crossed off in that journal. SARK inspired my dream journals with this question: *Why Dream?*

> "Life is a difficult assignment. We are fragile creatures, expected to function at high rates of speed, and asked to accomplish great and small things each day. These daily activities take enormous amounts of energy. Most things are out of our control. We are surrounded by danger, frustration, grief, and insanity as well as love, hope, ecstasy, and wonder. Being fully human is an exercise in humility, suffering, grace, and great humor. Things and people all around us die, get broken, or are lost. There is no safety or guarantees. The way to accomplish the

assignment of truly living is to engage fully, richly, and deeply in the living of your dreams. We are made to dream and to live those dreams."[99]

I believe it is more important than ever for women to dream—and dream BIG! If you don't become crystal clear on what you want, you will probably end up with a mediocre life. When we begin to identify what we want and don't want in our lives, we gradually change our consciousness.

For instance, before I met my husband, I composed a list of 45 things I REQUIRED IN A MAN BEFORE I WOULD EVEN BOTHER. *Guess what?* That exact man showed up a few years later without spending a moment looking for him. I just failed to mention a *location* and ended up with an amazing guy halfway around the world!

Mary Oliver challenged us with these words:

> "Tell me, what is it you plan to do with your one wild and precious life?"

My journals are where my dreams begin. It is magical to see them come into fruition and mark how far I have come. Keeping a journal is a gift to yourself—and possibly to others if you chose to share it.

---

[99] Sark. *Make Your Creative Dreams Real: A Plan for Procrastinators, Perfectionists, Busy People, and People Who Would Really Rather Sleep.* Atria Books; 2009.

Take Care of your Teeth

The health of your mouth correlates to your general physical health.[100] Therefore, if you are not taking good care of your teeth, now is the time to start.

Brushing and flossing are drilled into most of us since we were young, but neither is enough. And if you have had major dental work done, you know it can be very costly.

An inexpensive addition to your dental hygiene regime is oil pulling. If you have not tried oil pulling, I highly recommend it. This is an ancient practice with numerous benefits. Aside from promoting fresh breath and overall health, oil pulling can also be used for any dental aches and pains you may have. I also have used it successfully with headaches and migraines.

I start most days with a glass of lemon water, followed immediately with 20 minutes of oil pulling with organic coconut oil. Just put about 2 teaspoons of oil in your mouth and swish it around for 20 minutes. Spit it out into the trash can (not the sink, as it can clog) and then rinse your mouth out.

If you are not used to keeping oil in your mouth, you may have to work up to this with smaller increments. Any sort of oil can be used—but I prefer coconut oil for the mild taste.

You can read or check your emails with the oil in your mouth. Just be sure to swish it around so every area is saturated. When you are done, spit the remaining oil into the garbage or compost. Your mouth will feel cleaner instantly, and over time, your mouth and overall health with improve. I have not had any cavities since I began this practice. During the years where I was a single mom with no dental insurance, it helped me tremendously.

---

[100] Vander Stoep, Carol. *Mouth Matters:How Your Mouth Ages Your Body and What YOU Can Do About It.* Ianua Publishing; 2013.

Rewire Your Brain

Many of us have lived through years of trauma. Jane Caputi summed this up very well:

> "What is acted out on the female body parallels the larger practices of domination, fragmentation, and conquest against the earth body, which is being polluted, strip-mined, deforested, and cut up into parcels of private property. Equally, this pattern points to the fragmentation of the psyche, which ultimately underlies and enables all of this damage."[101]

Putting our psyches back together must become one of biggest priorities. It is not always easy to do though with the demands put on women. We must de-clutter our lives ruthlessly, beginning with refusing to take on work that it is not ours.

I spent about a year with severe brain fog, which really limited what I was able to do. When you suffer from memory loss, you often don't realize it at first because it tends to come on slowly. My daughter was the person who helped me see that I had a problem. I literally was not remembering very simple things and it was annoying her to no end. A year into my Norwegian studies, I finally acknowledged that my brain was just not working like it used to. I put her healing first and foremost.

I began resting more, taking supplements and getting back into a solid exercise and yoga routine. I read a lot of books about brain health, watched many webinars and read just about every article I could get ahold of. I have cut down on most of the supplements I took during that time to get back on track—but have realized that my brain functions much better when I take Ginkgo Biloba, get enough sleep and exercise.

---

[101] Caputi, Jane. *Age of Sex Crime*. Popular Press; 1987.

One thing I learned was that most of the 'safe' medications we use for pain management are anything but harmless. I had used Ibuprofen and Excedrin in excess to manage my pain for years. I had also taken Topamax to manage my migraines—and Benadryl and other over the counter sleeping pills for insomnia during my most stressful years. In excess, these pills have severe side effects, which can include memory loss.[102] I had stopped taking the Topamax years ago,[103] but I made a commitment to myself to get off the others as well. I now have to be nearly dying before I will ingest one of these pills.

Another thing I realized when I moved to Norway is that they don't pop those pills like candy here. My husband had never taken cold medicine well into his early 50's and has rarely taken a pain reliever for a headache. In addition, these medications are much costlier here in this country with socialized medicine. A box of 10 Ibuprofen costs about $12 here. I could buy a bottle of 500 pills for about $8 at Costco in America. The price difference alone speaks volumes.

If you are noticing a reduction in your brain function, there are supplements that can help. Dr. Mark Hyman has an excellent protocol up on his website, based on his book, *The UltraMind Solution: The Simple Way to Defeat Depression, Overcome Anxiety, and Sharpen Your Mind.*

I have come to believe that nothing is more important than women becoming healthy in mind and body. I now eat, supplement and move with the primary intention of supporting my brain health. I also create space just to sit and do nothing— and take walks to clear my mind. If your brain doesn't work properly, nothing else will.

---

[102] Mercola, Joseph Dr. "11 Surprising Factors That Mess With Your Memory." Mercola.com; September 18, 2014.

[103] Stanton, Angela PhD. "Topamax: The Drug with 9 Lives." *Hormones Matter;* September 10, 2015.

Don't Hold Your Anger In

Do you know what happens when you tell someone you're angry? You're not angry anymore. I used to be the master of holding it in. Now I'm not afraid to slam a few things down on the table with impact and say, *I'm not happy with you right now and here's why.* The anger usually dissipates as soon as I open my mouth.

If you find yourself being interrupted by a jerk who doesn't get it, save your breath and get some exercise. The simple act of walking away will either give them some time to process, or allow you to decide if this is a person who is even worth your time.

Holding in anger can hurt your health. Gabor Maté wrote, that "Sometimes the biggest impetus to healing can come from jump-starting the immune system with a burst of long-suppressed anger. Anger, or the healthy experience of it, is one of the seven A's of healing."[104] Women are at a disadvantage here because it is generally not socially acceptable for females to display anger.

Soraya Chemaly's book, *Rage Becomes Her: The Power of Women's Anger,* should be on everyone's book list. As Adrienne Rich wrote, "Most women have not even been able to touch this anger, except to drive it inward like a rusted nail."

It took decades before I was finally able to touch my anger—and it was a process, not so much one event. Today, I speak my anger when it comes. This feels so much better than the weight I carried around with me during my earlier years. I have come to realize that no one really cares when you are angry—and holding it in is both toxic to you while simultaneously benefiting the patriarchy. The expression of anger can create rapid change. Sometimes an asshole is just the impetus you need to start a movement.

---

[104] Maté, Gabor. *When the Body Says No: Understanding the Stress-Disease Connection.* Wiley; 2011.

Get Enough Sleep

Sleep is something you should never be stingy with, but most people don't get enough of it. As I get older, I have noted that I really do not function without 8 solid hours.

If you want to sleep well, keep your room cool and dark. Turn your WiFi off at night. Limit your electronic exposure after dinner. And don't drink alcohol before bed. Even one drink can severely disrupt your REM sleep.[105]

I still have some unresolved trauma remaining in my body, so sleep is sometimes difficult for me—particularly if there is any additional stress in my life at the moment. My life is not in chronic stress-mode like it used to be—but I can default to that if something triggers me and I let it go unchecked.

I have found that keeping a bottle of lavender essential oil is helpful to me during the night if I wake up. I also can reset myself by touching my husband or dog, connecting to some of their energy. I often joke with my husband about sex being my sleeping pill—and recommend that as well if it has that effect on you. Most nights, my husband gives me a full body massage beforehand to relax into the night. A cup of tea or a hot bath are also good rituals. Anything you can do to create a nighttime ritual to let your body know it is time to sleep will help you sleep better.

---

[105] Porter, William. *Alcohol Explained*. Createspace; 2015.

Give Yourself a Break

Most of us were not taught to listen to our bodies from childhood. It is something I have had to teach myself. I used to be sick more than I was well. I would push myself constantly and put everyone else first. Recently I started to feel a cold coming on, but I had a meeting at my daughter's school that night that I was supposed to attend. In the past, I would have reluctantly gone and been sick for 2 weeks. I felt bad for not going, but the next morning when I woke up feeling better, I knew it was worth it. I still have to work on my guilt at times—especially when it comes to my children—but having a healthy mother is more important than attending a meeting I can get notes on later from the teacher or another parent.

Humans are not machines. We are not meant to be 'on' 24/7. Your body needs regular breaks, both during the day and during the week. Try to take off at least one day a week to do nothing. Maya Angelou wrote: "Every person needs to take one day away. A day in which one consciously separates the past from the future. Jobs, family, employers, and friends can exist one day without any one of us, and if our egos permit us to confess, they could exist eternally in our absence. Each person deserves a day away in which no problems are confronted, no solutions searched for. Each of us needs to withdraw from the cares which will not withdraw from us."[106]

In Norway, pretty much everything is closed on Sunday, so I have learned to do my shopping the days before. We also have many more holidays, where everything is closed for days at a time. We have about 5 days off for both Christmas and Easter! And most people get a month off in July, in addition to generous time off for sickness and the needs of children. Coming from 40 years of going 24-7, it took me a few years to get used to all this. Life moves at a slower pace here, and I have come to really appreciate that.

---

[106] Angelou, Maya. *Wouldn't Take Nothing for My Journey Now.* Bantam; 1994.

An Orgasm a Day...

I believe we still have a lot of sexual hang-ups due to the influence of capitalism and patriarchy. Most women have so much on their to-do lists that sex seems like a chore and an orgasm like a luxury. Silvia Federici noted, "In capitalism, sex can exist but only as a productive force at the service of procreation and the regeneration of the waged/male working and as a mean of social appeasement and compensation for the misery of everyday existence."[107]

We must begin to teach our daughters to love and celebrate their bodies and their sexuality. So often, girls grow up surrounded by shame—whether it is about their changing bodies, their blood or masturbation—we still don't allow girls the same freedom we grant boys. Most Sex Ed programs don't even teach about female orgasm—or even the clitoris for that matter.

I think it's also important to consider how many women don't enjoy their sexuality (or don't experience orgasm) because of the various forms of abuse we suffer throughout our lifetimes. As someone who has been there, please remember that this does not have to be a life sentence.

If you are feeling low on sexual energy or disconnected from your yoni, my Reiki Goddess friend Sol Jonassen gave me an exercise recently that has been working wonders. I usually have a high sex drive and active sex life but it had been waning recently because we had been doing massive home repairs and our entire house was upside down. In any case, this may help you too.

Sit in a meditative position and inhale all the way down to your belly. Hold the breath until you are ready to release it, and exhale. Then repeat, but go all the way down into your yoni or root chakra

---

[107] Federici, Silvia. *Witches, Witch-Hunting, and Women.* PM Press; 2018.

—while doing a Kegel exercise—and hold the breath there. Concentrate on your vulva and feel the energy return there. Exhale and feel the surge of energy go back up through your crown chakra. Every time you inhale, feel the breath exhilarating your yoni. Repeat about 10 times. I felt my sexual energy come right back and have added it to my daily practices.

I know very few women who are completely comfortable talking openly about masturbation. But here's the thing: Females need to have orgasms too—and men are not always helpful in this way. Regular orgasms are good for physical and mental health—and can also help with pain relief. I used orgasm for migraine relief for years—as well as for cramps and back pain relief.

An orgasm is like a reset button. When my brain shuts down, oftentimes I realize I haven't had an orgasm for a few days. I stop what I am doing and lock myself in my room.

I don't use plastics in my vulva anymore as I don't believe they are good for her—and they certainly are not good for Mother Earth. So, my husband hand-carved a replica of his penis from an Asherah branch several years ago for my birthday. Someday soon I would also like to purchase a crystal wand, as I know many women who have both experienced great pleasure—and healing from these.

Pleasure has not been a consideration for most women for a long time. As a result, women don't have enough orgasms. This is both a statistical fact and something I have reflected on in my own life. The orgasm gap is a real thing.

> "In one study examining about 800 college students, a 52% orgasm gap was found. That is, 39 percent of women and 91 percent of men said that they usually or always experienced orgasm in partnered sex. This study didn't ask the context of the sex, but another study with 15,000 college students found that the orgasm gap is larger in

hookup sex than in relationship sex. Still, in college student committed relationships, there is still a 17% orgasm gap. Strikingly similar statistics were found in a survey of about 3,000 single women and men in the U.S. ranging from 18 to 65 years old. When having sex with a familiar partner, women said they have an orgasm 63% of the time; men said 85% of the time."[108]

The author also notes that there is an "orgasm gap between women who identify as lesbian versus straight. Lesbian women have significantly more orgasms than straight women."[109] I have certainly found sex with women to be much more egalitarian. How often do *men* have sex without an orgasm?

I decided a long time ago that I will absolutely not have sex with anyone who does not make my pleasure mandatory.

Orgasms are powerful, cleansing and free—and I love them!

---

[108] Mintz Ph.D., Laurie. "The Orgasm Gap: Simple Truth & Sexual Solutions." *Pyschology Today;* October 4, 2015.
[109] Mintz Ph.D., Laurie. "The Orgasm Gap: Simple Truth & Sexual Solutions." *Pyschology Today;* October 4, 2015.

Cleanse Regularly

Due to all the environmental toxins in our world today, I feel very strongly that to live well (and feel well) we have to go above and beyond what our parents and grandparents did to stay healthy.

I put together this cleansing protocol for my sister-friend Tamara and decided to share it here as well. This is what I do personally to cleanse. I recommend cleansing at least 2-4 times a year. This might sound extreme, but even simple things can really whack out your liver. For instance, we bought an old house that we have been remodeling. It has taken far longer than I ever dreamed it would—and my husband is the gung-ho, rambling project sort of guy. I realized that we have been painting, pretty much non-stop, for 7 months! That is some toxicity right there, even with lots of open windows!

Even the cleaning supplies that many people use in their homes are toxic. That is beyond the scope of this book, but I suggest all of us try to keep our homes, and our bodies, as toxin-free as possible. This is the protocol I use to stay healthy.

Cleansing Protocol

Have one large cup of water with half a lemon squeezed in as soon as you get out of bed. Save the other half for bedtime.

Next, do the oil pulling I mentioned earlier in the teeth chapter. This is cleansing for your entire body.

Eat one (thoroughly washed) organic apple. If you cannot afford organic apples, peel the skin off your apple—there are too many toxins to scrub out of the skin.

You can either skip breakfast and lunch and then have a moderate dinner—supplementing with juicing and smoothies—or just use those in between as snacks and try to eat lighter. Try to have a salad with lunch and dinner with a lemon/olive oil dressing. My go-to dressing is just half olive oil, half lemon juice with a clove of finely chopped garlic and salt and pepper to taste. I drink the leftover dressing straight from my bowl, much to the dismay of many of my dinner guests!

The **vegetable juice** that I generally make includes:

> 3 celery stocks
> 4 large carrots
> 1 clove of garlic
> an inch of ginger root
> turmeric root
> handful of brussel sprouts
> 1 beet
> half of a cucumber
> 1 hot red pepper (optional – will be *spicy!*)
> handful of fresh cilantro

I also just often use whatever I have in my fridge. I have very little waste, as I also am always making broth. (For instance, you can take the stem of the celery and make broth, or the apple cores from the apples you ate first thing in the morning can go into your juice.) You can compost what comes out of the juicer.

The **smoothie recipe** I use is as follows:

> 2 bananas
> 1 bag of frozen organic blueberries (can also be mixed with cherries and other berries)
> handful of fresh cilantro
> 1 grated avocado seed
> juice from 1 lime
> water as needed

This will make 2 large smoothies. You can either share with your family or save the rest for later.

If you don't have a blender or juicer, you can still do the cleanse, either by supplementing outside of your home at juice shops or eating more whole fruits and veggies. For many years, I could not afford a blender, a juicer or juice shops. That kept me from taking better care of myself. I made sure my kids got fruit, but I often went without so they could have it. Do the best you can with what you have at the moment. You have to start somewhere, and your physical health must become a top priority. Just keep taking little steps until you get where you want to be. *Everything* counts!

If you aren't able to do smoothies or juicing, I would eat the following each day between meals:

> 3 organic apples
> 2 bananas
> as many organic berries as you can.
> 5 celery stalks
> as many salads and fresh veggies as possible

At bedtime, take the other lemon with a large glass of water – probably 30 minutes before so you don't have to get up to go to the bathroom in the night. Sleep as much as possible. Avoid sugar, alcohol, caffeine, gluten, dairy, processed food, trans fats, processed salt, and any sort of unprescribed medication that is not absolutely necessary (like Ibuprofen, cold medicine, sleeping pills). You may get a slight detox headache in about 4 days in. Best to rest and use a cold compress and peppermint oil on your temples if you can.

Continue for 7-10 days. Repeat every 3 months, or more if you like! This is not about dieting, but about giving your body a break once in a while. She works very hard to keep you healthy—give her the love and respect she deserves back.

WARNING: This is not advisable or pregnant or lactating women. IF YOU HAVE DIABETES or other illnesses—ASK YOUR DOCTOR!

Breathe

Margo Anand explained that, "Most of us live on a beggar's ration of air. The average person inhales one pint of air per breath, while our lungs can actually contain seven pints when fully expanded. This is one of the reasons that the range and depth of our experiences disappoint our longings."[110]

I began to notice the importance of breath while writing *New Love* with Arna Baartz. At that point, I was slacking on the Kundalini Yoga practice I had cultivated during my divorce, despite the fact that it literally saved my sanity! *How crazy is that?*! I am pleased to say that I am back on board, and working on my breathing, yoga and meditation every day. We all have days—and sometimes years—where we do things against our own self-interest, even when we know better. All you can do is get back on track and keep moving in the right direction.

The meditations I use with my daily breath work are quite simple.

I am healthy. I am happy. I am holy.[111]

I love and approve of myself.[112]

If you prefer a more guided meditation type of thing where someone does the talking and imagining for you, my favorite one is available on Patricia Lynn Reilly's website.[113]

I have asked my dear friend Susan Morgaine to write this bit, as she is far more an expert on this subject than me. And now, I turn things over to Susan...

---

[110] Anand, Margo. *The Art of Sexual Ecstasy. Jeremy P.* Tarcher; 1988.
[111] Kundalini Meditation.
[112] Hay, Louise. *You Can Heal Your Life*. Hay House; 1984.
[113] Reilly, Patricia Lynn. "Home is Always Waiting." Imagine a Woman International; 2010.

PRANAYAMA FOR PATRIARCHAL COPING
By Susan Morgaine (Devta Kaur)

PRANA. BREATH. LIFE FORCE.

It's no secret that—for women, people of color, children, and the LGBT+ community—living under patriarchy is a struggle. There is no denying that we are devalued, demeaned, de-humanized, and destroyed little by little at the core of who we are. For some, this means death—as we are killed by our partners, by officers of the law and those in authority.

As you will see throughout this book, there are many techniques for coping with the daily struggle.

One of these is pranayama, conscious breathing. Prana is your breath, what you bring in; it is your life force, for without breath, you would cease to be.

Your breath is a fundamental tool in being able to control your emotions and your mood. It can reduce stress and tension; give you clarity of thought; increase focus; increase patience; reduce and prevent toxins in your body that we are continuously bringing in via food, drink and air. It does this while also expanding your lung capacity; cleansing your blood and relaxing and calming you. Just a slight change in the breath creates a huge impact.

To have a daily pranayama/meditation practice, it is optimum to have a designated place in your home. You can have a small altar or just some flowers, incense, and a candle. There is some wonderful meditation music out there; find some that speaks to your spirit. Most importantly, shut off your phone. Let this become your special place—a place of quiet and serenity.

Your candles are lit, incense wafting through the room. Sit yourself comfortably in easy pose, cross-legged on the floor. If you are unable to sit on the floor, a straight-backed chair works well. You want to be comfortable, but it is important that the spine be straight.

You want to center yourself, to be in the moment, in that time, in that place. Bring your hands into prayer position at your chest, or you may simply rest your hands on your knees. Close your eyes and gently roll them up so that they are focused upon your third eye, that space between your eyebrows in the middle of your forehead. Begin to slowly and deeply inhale and exhale. Take your time, don't rush through it. Really feel each breath; on your breath. Now, with each inhale, bring into your body a sense of peace, a sense of calm. Let it infuse your entire being, beginning with the heart chakra and working outward. With each exhale, release any stress, tension or negativity you are holding within your body, even that of which you may not even be consciously aware. Allow yourself to let it go.

You can continue this for as long as you are comfortable. If monkey-mind thoughts come calling, gently push them away and continue with the breath. When you are finished, take several deep breaths while stretching your arms up to the skies.

This long, deep breathing is for when you have the time to sit and focus on that precious conscious breath. This breath can also be used as a "quick fix." Find someplace quiet and breathe in the positive and breathe out the negative. The perfect thing with conscious breathing, is that it is always with you. Calm is only a breath away.

I will be sharing with you some breath techniques, all of which come from Kundalini Yoga, as taught by Yogi Bhajan, which I have been honored and proud to be teaching for 20 years.

****

For Calmness – Inhale for a count of 4 and exhale for a count of 8. This is a good breath to practice when you are feeling stressed or anxious. It produces a calm and relaxed state of being.

For Relaxation – Breathe only through your left nostril. The left side of your body relates to the moon, which is the calming and receptive side of your body. For women, this will connect you to the feminine energy of the moon.

"U" Breathing – Purifying breath. Try to visualize the path of the breath. Inhale and visualize light flowing down the same side of the nostril, down the spine to your first chakra. As you hold the breath, feel and see the light swirling and growing at the base of the spine.

One Minute Breath – Inhale for 20 seconds, hold for 20 seconds, exhale for 20 seconds. There will be an immediate calming of anxiety, fear and tension.

Stress Relief and Cleansing of Past Emotions – Hands are in front of your heart center in a tent - fingers touching; palms not. Long, slow deep breathing, segmented inhaling for a count of 5, suspend the breath for a count of 5 and segmented exhaling for a count of 5. Eyes should be focused at the tip of the nose.

Anti-Stress Breathing – Sit in easy pose (on floor, legs crossed, spine straight) or sit in a straight-backed chair. It is important that your spine be straight, your shoulders back and your head level. Press the tips of your thumbs and little fingers together. Extend your arms out somewhere between your heart and belly button, arms slightly bent at elbows. Focus your eyes on the tip of your nose (if this makes you dizzy, close your eyes). Inhale through the mouth with a long, deep and powerful breath and exhale through the nose. Then inhale through the nose and exhale through the mouth. It may take a little bit of time to start to work, but it will calm inner stress and tension. Continue for at least 3 minutes.

Mudra for Preventing Stress – *Try this one to prevent stress from even starting. (The Sanskrit word "mudra," in yoga, is a hand position. Mudra is a Sanskrit word.) Sit in easy pose with a straight spine. Relax your arms, and bend your elbow, bringing your forearms in front of you and parallel to the ground. Bring your hands, palms up, to meet in front of you, a little above your belly button. Rest the back of the left hand in the palm of the* right hand. Keep your fingers together and straight. Your breath will be long, slow and deep and through the nostrils only. Do for at least 3 minutes.

****

All of these breaths can be done for any length of time, and/or are available for immediate use. There's nothing wrong with finding a quiet spot or even a public restroom to focus on your breath and re-gain control of yourself or a situation.

While nothing is a miracle, I am positive that, with practice of these breaths, you will find yourself feeling calmer and better able to cope with some of the injustices and atrocities that are present in the patriarchal world.

Sat Nam!
(Truth is My Identity)

Make Time for Yoga

Gurmukh's *Kundalini Yoga* DVD has changed my life. I do some version of it every day and strive to do the entire thing at least 5 days a week. I used to be turned off by yoga because I found it boring to stay in poses indefinitely. This is a very active routine that your entire body—and brain—will thank you for!

The DVD came out in 2004 so you may have to find a used version at this point. If you don't have an extra $10 lying around just now —don't wait to start. There are thousands of free yoga sessions on YouTube, including some fun ones with Gurmukh!

Better yet, get into a class with a regular community of yogis to support you. My schedule and to-do list are beyond insane, but this is on my personal to-do list for this year. I know being in a class will help me tremendously and stretch me beyond what I can do at home alone.

If you have children and think you can't do yoga anymore, look into Yoga Pretzels (Yoga Cards) by Tara Guber and Leah Kalish. I used these with my children when they were young and also used them in several programs I led with young girls. Whenever my group would become too unruly, I'd pull out the deck and let them choose 3-4 cards. The girls absolutely loved it and would often fight over who got to choose a card.

It's not exactly the same to do yoga with young children, but sometimes you have to work with where you're at. These cards saved my sanity when I was a single mom.

Exercise Everyday

This one does not come easy to many of us (including me) but it is important to work in. I walk nearly everywhere and have a small dog who needs to go out several times a day—so I don't make much of a concerted effort, but it is something I am trying to incorporate into my daily routine.

When you experience trauma, it is stored in your body. Exercise helps you release some of that trauma and regenerates your cells. Bodywork can also be very effective, but exercise is free.

Our bodies were not meant to be sedentary. Every time you get up and move, you are shaking things up a bit. I make it a point to get out and walk twice during my workday and take another break for yoga.

My husband is a decade older than me, but much more fit. On top of biking to work every day, he does Thai Boxing and MMA Training. I will know I have come a long way in my healing process when I make as much time for exercise as he does.

Put Sisterhood First

If you don't have good sister-friends in your life, it is time to find some. And I mean in real life, not just online. Online friends are wonderful, but it is not the same thing to have someone who can be at your house holding you while you sob when everything falls apart.

I struggled with this when I moved to Bergen. I had lived in Portland for 40 years and had many long-term friendships I cherished. Part of me didn't want to make new friends. I didn't realize what a mistake that had been for at least a year. I have a wonderful husband and great kids. I thought that was enough with the friends I had from afar. I realize now that I need my sisters locally. Now I make a concerted effort to schedule things every week with women who live nearby. I also try to participate in Women's Circles, book clubs and other events for women whenever possible.

Inga Muscio wrote that, "Women choose to be catty, cruel, prejudiced, competitive or jealous of each other partly because we grow up learning that negative behavior towards women is perfectly acceptable, and partly because it is a difficult task to see ourselves in our perceptions. Seeing ourselves requires effort and commitment. This unwillingness to see ourselves is greatly exacerbated by the fact that we, quite often, do not see even a remote semblance of ourselves in the images of women commonly found in our society."[114]

All too often, women focus on their differences instead of what they have in common. This is especially true online, which is why I think face-to-face interaction is so important. Feminism has become too fragmented. I can't tell you how many times someone has tried to tell me how they can't stand someone because they disagree with 2% of their ideology. Sonia Johnson wrote that,

---

[114] Muscio, Inga. *Cunt: A Declaration of Independence.* Seal Press; 2002.

"Once we understand that patriarchy is totally dependent upon our mistrusting and thwarting and hurting one another, and that for this reason we have been deliberately, thoroughly, and fiercely indoctrinated from birth to hate and to hurt women, surely we can forgive one another and learn to resist the most central and deadly of all patriarchal mandates."[115]

Personally, I am not interested in people's disagreements anymore and tend to stay out of them unless someone is being bullied. Malcolm X said, "Don't be in such a hurry to condemn a person because s/he doesn't do what you do or think as you think or as fast. There was a time when you didn't know what you know today." We are all learning and growing. I am not the same person I was 10 years ago. 25 years ago, you would not recognize me at all!

Not to mention... the world would be a very boring place if we all thought the same things. I think it is time we give each other a break. Let's take a big collective breath and start fresh.

Phyllis Chesler made 9 suggestions in her groundbreaking book, *Woman's Inhumanity to Women*. The last 3 are my favorite:

9. Do Not Gossip
Do not initiate gossip about another woman; if you hear gossip, do not pass it on. Let it stop with you. It's perfectly all right to talk about a woman when she is not present as long as she is someone you like, love, care about, and if what you are saying will not damage her reputation or ruin her life. It is not all right to punish and sabotage another woman whom you may envy or fear by slandering her or by turning other women against her.

---

[115] Johnson, Sonia. *Going Out of Our Minds: The Metaphysics of Liberation.* Crossing Pr.; 1987.

8. **No Woman Is Perfect: Apologize When You've Made a Mistake and Then Move On.**

If you behave badly, apologize directly and move on. Cut yourself some slack and cut the next woman some slack too. If she has slandered or sabotaged you, talk to her about it directly; deal with it quickly. Do not let it fester.

9. **Treat Women Respectfully.**

Finally, even if we disagree with another woman, we must do so respectfully, kindly. We must cultivate the concept of an "honourable opponent." We should not automatically demonize our opponents or competitors. Women are not obligated to "love" or "hate" each other. We do not even need to "like" each other. I am suggesting that women treat each other in a civilized manner. Finally, women might learn how to thank other women for each small act of kindness – as opposed to expecting everything from other women and being angry when we don't get it.[116]

We also must do a better job of supporting women of color and those who are poor or disadvantaged in other ways. If you cannot be bothered to fight for the rights of your disadvantaged sisters, you probably will not get very far with your own liberation. We are all tied together in this. As Audre Lorde wrote, "I am not free while any woman is unfree, even when her shackles are very different from my own. And I am not free as long as one person of Color remains chained. Nor is any of you."[117]

We must begin to listen to our sisters who are most hurt by colonialism, racism and militarism. I would venture to say that if more of us invited our local refugees to our dinner table, none of us would tolerate another day of war anywhere in the world.

---

[116] Chesler, Phyllis. *Woman's Inhumanity to Women.* Chicago Review Press; 2009.

[117] Lorde, Audre. "The Uses of Anger: Women Responding to Racism." *Sister Outsider: Essays and Speeches*. Ten Speed Press; Reprint edition, 2007.

bell hooks made an important distinction:

> "Solidarity is not the same as support. To experience
> solidarity, we must have a community of interests, shared
> beliefs and goals around which to unite, to build
> Sisterhood. Support can be occasional. It can be given and
> just as easily withdrawn. Solidarity requires sustained,
> ongoing commitment."[118]

Who are the women in your life? Do they all look the same, speak the same language, and practice the same religion? If so, it may be time to take a close look at yourself and learn about other women. Don't expect these women to teach you. Go out and buy their books and educate yourself first. There are some suggestions at the end of this book if you don't know where to start.

There is so much information available now. There are no more excuses for racism or isolation. As my dear friend and activist Desiree Jordan says, "Choosing to close your eyes to racism IS accepting your own part in an 'organized resistance' to equality and justice."

Expand your circle of sisters. Be a real friend to each of them by listening and helping when you are able to. There is a reason why the sister-relationship is so powerful. We grow up together through the good and bad times and learn how to have each other's backs.

One of my earlier regrets in life was not being able to give my daughter a sister to grow up with. The sister-friends I have made over the last decade have alleviated this sadness and shown me that sisterhood goes far beyond the biological bond. I believe we

---

[118] hooks, bell. *Feminist Theory: From Margin to Center.* South End Press; 2000.

can have sister relationships with many different women—and our lives will be richer for it.

Sisterhood is not superficial. Hence, it sometimes gets messy, complicated, dirty and loud. I don't know about you, but I fought with my sisters growing up—and occasionally still do today. Don't fear arguments or disagreements. Don't be afraid to get real. Learn to speak your truth and listen to others do the same. Master how to give generously and receive gracefully. Don't settle for friends or acquaintances—or even pretending everything is *just fine*. With a sister, you can sob recklessly and laugh until you snort or pee. Go all the way and develop some sister relationships. A friend may cry when you're gone but a sister will hold your hand as you're dying and watch out for your children until she can't. There is no replacement for a sister.

Don't Give Men Authority in Your Life

Your father or husband is not the boss of you. You are.

You are not a child anymore. You don't need your husband's permission to live. I have seen far too many women defer to their husband—even on minor things. In my own life, I waited for my father's approval until my late 30's. Sometimes I still crave it, even though I know better.

Some of us are not even aware that we are doing this until we stop. When I rather suddenly refused to do this anymore, some men in my life became enraged in a way they could not put words to. Patriarchal religion sets us up to worship at the feet of men to our own detriment. However, when you begin to study just how that was accomplished, it becomes trickier for men to maintain their stronghold. Jean Shinoda Bolen wrote:

> "Successive waves of invasions by the Indo-Europeans began the dethronement of the Great Goddess. The dates when these waves began are given by various authorities as between 4500 B.C. and 2400 B.C. The goddesses were not completely suppressed but were incorporated into the religion of the invaders.
>
> The invaders imposed their patriarchal culture and their warrior religion on the conquered people. The Great Goddess became the subservient consort of the invaders' gods, and attributes or power that originally belonged to a female divinity were expropriated and given to a male deity. Rape appeared in myths for the first time, and myths arose in which the male heroes slew serpents—symbols of the Great Goddess. And, as reflected in Greek mythology, the attributes, symbols, and power that were once invested in one Great Goddess were divided among many

goddesses. Mythologist Jane Harrison notes that the Great Mother goddess became fragmented into many lesser goddesses, each receiving attributes that once belonged to her."[119]

This is not an easy thing to break out of. We have been indoctrinated from birth to defer to men. Men are the default in everything, whether it be medicine, books, art or religion. Start by reading only female writers. You don't need the Bible or the Quran as the authority in your life. *You* are the authority in your life. You also don't need Hemingway or Faulkner clouding your view of yourself with their distorted thinking on women. Start reading female authors exclusively for a while and see how your reality shifts. As Audre Lorde wrote:

> "For the master's tools will never dismantle the master's house. They may allow us temporarily to beat him at his own game, but they will never enable us to bring about genuine change. And this fact is only threatening to those women who still define the master's house as their only source of support."[120]

Buy and hang female art in your home. This will also help to shift your reality. We have primarily art by females hung in our home— except for our dear friend Ljudmil Nikolov, and a few pieces by my husband and his father. I have also started collecting Goddess figurines and other woman-affirming art. For me, having this art prominently displayed throughout my home is critically important, especially as someone who was brought up in a fundamentalist church. Carol P. Christ wrote that "Images of the Goddess help to

[119] Bolen,Jean Shinoda M.D., *Goddesses in Every Woman: Powerful Archetypes in Women's Lives*. Harper 2nd ed; 2014.
[120] Lorde, Audre. "The Uses of Anger: Women Responding to Racism." *Sister Outsider: Essays and Speeches*. Ten Speed Press; Reprint edition, 2007.

break the hold of 'male control' that has shaped our images not only of God, but of all significant power in the universe."[121] I want my daughter and sons to grow up with these images—and to influence the psyche of every single person who enters my home.

I went a step further and took my daughter on a Goddess Pilgrimage to Crete with Carol Christ last fall. I wanted her to see first-hand the rich Goddess HERstory and enable her to have a different vision of her life than I did at 12-years-old.

Following my own ethics in terms of how I raise my daughter has been one of my greatest challenges. It is not always easy to let her have her emotions and feelings. A girl who remains full of herself is feared in this world—and we both have experienced backlash at times. That said, I have seen so many little girls lose their spunk and fearlessness over the years. It is as if the light has been drained from their eyes. I recognize those eyes in myself. Luce Irigaray wrote, "To become means fulfilling the wholeness of what we are capable of being... But as long as woman lacks a divine made in her image she cannot establish her subjectivity or achieve a goal of her own. She lacks an ideal that would be her goal or path in becoming."

Sometimes my daughter 'gets back at me' for the way I have raised her when I revert to patriarchal top-down parenting methods instead of those based on mutual respect. She reminds me, "You're the one who told me that I AM the authority in my own life." I have to smile and say, "You're right." I have no doubt that she will never put up with nonsense—from anyone, including me.

It is my belief that we should raise children to become autonomous adults—not robots. I believe when parenting shifts

---

[121] Christ, Carol P. *Rebirth of the Goddess: Finding Meaning in Feminist Spirituality.* Routledge; 1998.

culturally, we will have more people who are willing to rise up and resist the status quo. This is especially critical in regards to how we raise females. Chimamanda Ngozi Adichie wrote:

> "We teach girls to be likable, to be nice, to be false. And we do not teach boys the same. This is dangerous. Many sexual predators have capitalized on this. Many girls remain silent when abused because they want to be nice. Many girls spend too much time trying to be "nice" to people who do them harm. Many girls think of the "feelings" of those who are hurting them. This is the catastrophic consequence of likability. We have a world full of women who are unable to exhale fully because they have for so long been conditioned to fold themselves into shapes to make themselves likable."[122]

I don't want my daughter searching for male approval as a grown woman. This is something that took me years to overcome. Birthing her was the impetus for this change in myself.

We are all working through male-imposed patterns that do not serve us well. Mary Daly called this "Metapatterning—breaking through patriarchal patterns and Weaving our way out of male-ordered mazes."[123] Every time we read a book authored by a woman or hang art in our homes created by a female, we are breaking through these male ordered mazes. Some of us may take our entire lifetime to break free—other women may never even notice their chains. This is difficult work. Just remember that every time you break a rule, you are modeling how it can be done.

---

[122] Adichie, Chimamanda Ngozi. *Dear Ijeawele, or A Feminist Manifesto in Fifteen Suggestions.* Anchor; 2017.

[123] Daly, Mary. Websters' First New Intergalactic Wickedary of the English Language. Womens Pr Ltd; 1998.

Stop Supporting Men Financially

Years ago, I began to shift my purchases to women-owned businesses whenever possible. For years, I only read books by women, although I occasionally make an exception now.

One thing I feel very strongly about is that we must share with our sisters whenever we are able.

I have stopped giving my money to the church or the mosque or to Red Cross or any other large "humanitarian" organization. I prefer to share with women I know well in real life, but not always. When my children's father died, my friend Daylene set up a GoFundMe account for us to go home because we had no funds to do so. There are times in life when you can give, and there are times when you must swallow your pride and receive. Frankly, I think many females have a harder time with receiving.

Sharing doesn't have to be money though. It can be sharing the work and posts of other women on social media. It can be helping a single mother out by watching her kids so she can get a much-needed break. For me, it also means that I limit my sharing to mostly women—because they are the most disadvantaged under this system. Genevieve Vaughan wrote:

> "At present, white males are still the most successful purveyors of patriarchy. Through mechanisms such as the free market, they continue to dominate the global economy. It is therefore the responsibility of their caregivers, especially white women, together with white women's allies among women and men of color *and* white men, to turn against patriarchy and dismantle it from within. We must all cease rewarding bio-pathic behaviors

and systems. Women and men must stop nurturing patriarchy."[124]

It is also critically important that women stop providing free labor. Let me be clear here: if you are in an equal partnership where you are both sharing chores *and* money that is one thing. If your husband 'works' and controls all the money while you slave away at home and have no access to funds, it is time to stop working for him.

Unless you are in an abusive relationship where your safety is at risk, I would ask you to consider every single way you give your time away for free—and think about what works for you and what doesn't. I will never stop cooking—because I LOVE it. And I will never stop doing everything I can for my children. But I do expect them to contribute as well. I expect my husband and stepsons to put in their fair share too.

Men already control the vast majority of money and resources. They do not need our financial support or free labor. Save more of your money and free-time for yourself. You will be amazed at how much you can accomplish.

---

[124] Vaughan,Genevieve. *For-giving: A Feminist Criticism of Exchange.* Plain View Press; 1997.

Demand Maternity Leave

When I gave birth to my son 16 years ago, I literally walked back into my office 2 days later with him in his stroller to pick up my files. I resumed my regular 60-hour work-week from there and did not slow down again until I became pregnant with my daughter 3 years later. Working was an economic necessity for me and I did not have any leave available to me as a commissioned loan officer. However, by the time I became pregnant with my daughter, I could simply not do it anymore. My body is still paying for this.

Katherine Goldstein recently published a stirring article calling American women to action. "Since we live in the only industrialized country that doesn't mandate paid family leave, nearly 25% of mothers go back to work within two weeks of giving birth. To give you a sense of where human mothers fall on the legal protection hierarchy, it's illegal to separate a dog from her newborn pups before eight weeks in several states. Once we return to work, we unfortunately can expect anti-mom bias in hiring, pay and promotions. And, if a woman has a baby between the ages of 25 and 35, she can expect a lifetime of economic marginalization and diminished earnings."[125]

The lack of maternity leave in the United States is inhumane. We are so far behind the rest of the world, it is embarrassing. American women *should* be angry.

In Norway, women get 35-45 weeks of maternity leave, much of it paid. Men also can take paternity leave if they choose to. My husband took about a year with both of his boys, and I can still see all the ways that pays off in their relationships now as his sons

---

[125] Goldstein, Katherine. "American moms: let's stop feeling guilty and start getting mad." *The Guardian*; February 13, 2019.

enter early adulthood. Being a father means something here—far greater than just a name on a paper—and financial support if you are lucky enough to get it.

Systematic change can take time—but it must happen. Until then, we must support our sisters who have given birth. Show up with dinner, cake, coffee—and offer to hold the baby while she showers. Sometimes the little things can make all the difference. I remember rushing through my showers with my son in his car seat carrier so he would be safe. I don't think I had a proper shower until both my kids were over the age of 5.

We should encourage new fathers to actually *be* fathers.

I cannot remember my children's father doing much of anything to help me with our babies. On the few occasions that he actually changed a diaper, you'd think he deserved an award. (He did bring me good take-out food though—and for that I will always be grateful!)

We must raise the bar for fatherhood—considerably—in most of the world. And we must make it easier for mothers and children. As Stanley Greenspan, MD wrote, "If our society were truly to appreciate the significance of children's emotional ties throughout the first years of life, it would no longer tolerate children growing up, or parents having to struggle, in situations that cannot possibly nourish healthy growth." We must demand better ways to support parenting.

Demand Equal Pay

I am so tired of the having this discussion so many years later. Equal pay should be a reality, everywhere—right now.

While it is probably impracticable, I would love to see women everywhere walk off their jobs and create their own economies. Capitalist Patriarchy is fueled off the cheap (and often free) labor of females. The men who benefit need us far more than we need them. We must begin toward a shift in consciousness around this before we can even attempt to change it. We have been beating a dead horse for decades around this issue because we continue to provide free and cheap labor despite knowing how unfair and immoral it is.

I believe we can look to our Icelandic sisters for guidance here, as they still have one of the smallest pay gaps in the world. On October 24th 1975, Icelandic women went on strike for the day to "demonstrate the indispensable work of women for Iceland's economy and society"[126] and to "protest wage discrepancy and unfair employment practices."[127] Ninety percent of Iceland's female population participated in the strike, refusing to go to their jobs or do any housework. The parliament passed a law guaranteeing equal pay the following year.

In the meantime, here are some practical suggestions: Refuse to work one minute more than you are being paid for. Ask for a raise regularly. Require that your partner or son does his share around the house. If you have children, pay them equal allowances.[128]

---

[126] "Icelandic women strike for economic and social equality, 1975 | Global Nonviolent Action Database." *Global Nonviolent Action Database*. Swarthmore College.

[127] "The day the women went on strike." *The Guardian*. October 18, 2005.

[128] Chemaly, Soraya. "Even Little Kids Have a Wage Gap." *Salon*; August 15, 2013.

And while we are at it, let's really get to the heart of something that has been bugging me for a while within feminism itself.

While finishing this book and writing about the importance of equal pay and not giving away our time for free—it hit me pretty hard that I have been doing this in the name of feminism for the last 7 years. *Which ends today.* As Kate Northrup wrote, "If you can't see your value, the world doesn't give value back."[129]

We don't expect teachers and nurses to work without a salary. *Why is this so often the expectation with feminist work?*

I have lost track of the number of outstanding women who have given their lives to the cause—who still struggle every month. Barbara Mor and Monica Sjöö are particularly painful examples to me because of how many women have told me over and over again how much *The Great Cosmic Mother* changed their lives. The question that begs to be asks is, **what might these women have accomplished—for all of us—if they were not constricted by the realities of being poor?**

How can we possibly look at ourselves as anything other than exploiters if we expect these women to work their entire lives on our behalfs only to grow old in poverty—while we reap the benefits? This seems like the ultimate hypocrisy to me.

Surely, we could do better for our sisters and foremothers—at least going forward. We must begin to truly support feminist work.

---

[129] Northrup, Kate. *Money, A Love Story: Untangling Your Finances, Creating the Life You Really Want, and Living Your Purpose.* Hay House Inc.; 2013.

Fight for Child Support

When my ex-husband died, he owed me more than $46,000 in back child support. I lived many years of my children's lives without any child support, and we all suffered immensely for it. In the U.S. alone, there are billions of dollars of unpaid support—but it is rarely written about.[130] As Vanessa Olorenshaw writes, "When it comes to *women*, how far do patriarchal and exploitative capitalist values *rely* on women providing *unwaged* care, on which our society can freeload and from which it can wash its hands of financial responsibility?"[131]

We need a WORLDWIDE child support revolution.

I remember one night in particular, when things looked particularly bleak as to whether I'd get my past due child support. I sobbed on my husband's shoulder and cried out, "I don't want to live in a world where I can't get this money. I *won't* live in a world where I cannot get this money."

I finally received all my back support after my ex-husband died— mostly because I fought for it. I am probably about the most hated woman ever at the Multnomah County Child Support (Non)Enforcement office. But I kept checking in. I complained to the state office and the National one. I cast spells, sometimes every day. I imagined that money in my bank account. When it was finally there, I could hardly believe it!

I want ALL single mothers to receive full support payments, which is why I have been so open about how I finally got mine.

---

[130] Several years ago, we published an anthology that contains additional information on this entitled *Single Mothers Speak on Patriarchy*.

[131] Orenshaw, Vanessa. *Liberating Motherhood: Birthing the Purplestockings Movement*. Womancraft Publishing; 2016.

I want every mother to get her full child support payment every single month. I want all back child support, world-wide paid. **This will only happen when we support each other in demanding this.** No child should have to do without because of a selfish father. No mother should have to crucify herself because her ex wants to punish her.

Furthermore, those of us who are or have been single mothers, must find better ways of supporting ourselves in the meantime. Matriarchal researcher Heide Göttner-Abendroth recently suggested that young single mothers should form "matriarchal clans," which should include "older women as supporters and counselors and men who share maternal values."[132]

Initially I planned to name this chapter, 'Fight for Child Support if you are owed it.' But while editing, I realized this is part of the problem. We need ALL women to fight so that no woman or child is left without this critical financial support.

---

[132] Michael Caspar, Von. "Werben für neues Matriarchat." *Goettinger Tageblatt,* 05.10.2018. Google Translate was used to translate this article from the original German into English.

Build Your Own Village

The individualist nature of Capitalist Patriarchy hits women hardest—especially if they have young children. As Elizabeth Tenety noted recently:

> "It takes a village, but there are no villages. . . [mama,] you and I are not the problem at all. WE ARE DOING PLENTY. We may feel inadequate, but that's because we're on the front lines of the problem, which means we're the ones being hardest hit. We absorb the impact of a broken, still-oppressive social structure so that our children won't have to. That makes us heroes, not failures."[133]

I still feel worn out and exhausted from my years as a single mother. Some days, I am not sure if my health will ever fully recover, as much as I try to rectify that.

More than that, I know that my children suffered those years. Thankfully my mother helped us a lot. The world needs more grandmas—and more aunties.

Sometimes I think we are all just too tired to even try to connect anymore. Or we hold up unrealistic expectations about how clean our house must be before we invite someone over.

Frankly, I have never cared how clean or unclean someone's house was. I cared about the quality of the time that we spent together. We must begin to do whatever it takes to bring back a sense of community into our world.

---

[133] Tenety, Elizabeth. "American Mothers are Trying Harder Than Ever–So Why Do We Feel Like We're Failing?" *Medium*; February 6, 2019.

Adopt an Animal

Animals can be amazing additions to your family. We have a wonderful little mutt named Lily—who is my co-worker. I work at home, on the couch for the most part—and Lily snuggles up to me almost all-day-long. When she thinks I have been working too much, she scratches at my hands, so I literally can't type anything —and insists on a walk.

Dogs are also great when your kids aren't as cuddly anymore. Dogs love you no matter what. (But be good to them anyway. Dogs are kind souls and deserve that same love back.)

My daughter is going through puberty, which can be difficult. I notice that she is able to reset herself with Lily in a few minutes. No matter how bad her day has been, she can sit with Lily on their chair by the fireplace and reconnect to happiness and love.

Lily also seems to know intuitively when and where I am hurting. When I have cramps, she will lie on my tummy like a furry heating pad. When my back is hurting, she will lie there.

Dogs don't have to be expensive—in fact there are many who need good homes. My cousin spends her days (and nights) doing dog rescue—something I am very proud of her for.

If you don't have the time or money for a dog, borrow one from a neighbor! When our neighbor's dog died—and she missed him terribly—she started coming over to ask if she could walk our dog. That worked great for both of us. What dog couldn't use an extra walk?

We also have recently adopted a kitten, who I am absolutely in love with. Did you know that when a cat purrs, it can be healing to the human body and psyche? Purring has been linked to lowering stress and high-blood pressure, alleviating shortness of breath, lessening the chances of having a heart attack, and even healing bones.[134]

I have also realized that the purring works wonders for insomnia. One night, I could not sleep no matter what I did, and the cat came and slept on my head. Every time I would wake up, he would start purring again until I fell asleep. He has also helped me return more deeply to a meditative state. I often hold him near me, while breathing deeply with his purrs and connecting to something far greater than both of us.

I believe animals bring enormous joy, love, and healing into our lives.

---

[134] O'Connell, Rebecca. "The Healing Power of the Cat Purr." *Mental Floss;* May 5, 2015.

Engage in Fiber Arts

I learned how to sew as a teenager but was never great at it. Fortunately, boys and girls both learn how to knit and sew in school in Norway and my husband is much more precise than I am. As I mentioned, we purchased a fixer home last year—and the curtains were all extremely dated and dirty from cigarette smoke. We looked around for good deals on curtains, but I did not find what I wanted. We saved a lot of money by finding inexpensive fabric and making our own. I have always been a bit too impatient for sewing and knitting, but I am trying to overcome this because I value the outcome and the process.

I have several knitted items around my house that I treasure. My friend Summayah crocheted a gorgeous blanket that I use nearly every day. My daughter often wraps it around herself when she feels sick or sad. My friend Susan sent a beautiful scarf from the East Coast with a note that said it was the closest thing she could send to a hug—to wrap around myself. And my wonderful mother-in-law knitted so many pot holders that are now on their last legs, but I still cannot bring myself to toss out. I have used these in the process of creating so many meals over the last years. She also made two long rugs from my husband's confirmation outfit after he outgrew it. We have also displayed many of her banners—which bring us joy every day. I am saddened that I did not have more time with my mother-in-law before she passed. But I feel her presence very deeply in our home. What you create remains long after you are gone.

There are also numerous health benefits to knitting and crocheting. "Dr. Herbert Benson, a pioneer in mind/body medicine and author of *The Relaxation Response*, says that the repetitive action of needlework can induce a relaxed state like that associated with meditation and yoga. Once you get beyond the initial learning curve, knitting and crocheting can lower heart rate and blood pressure and reduce harmful blood levels of the stress hormone Cortisol."[135]

I also believe that many of these arts will allow women to remember the ancient ways of being. Meadow Colden, who hosts *The Woven Road* blog, writes that, "When we engage in fiber arts, we are creating something, but we are also participating in historic traditions tens of thousands of years old. You are not only making art for your soul and for future generations, you are embodying the work of our ancestors."

At this time, there is nothing more important than remembering their wisdom. When we slow our pace, we can reconnect with each stitch.

---

[135] Brody, Jane E. "The Health Benefits of Knitting." *New York Times;* January 25, 2016.

Gerda Lerner wrote that, "Women's history is the primary tool for women's emancipation."[136] Patriarchy has colonized our minds for thousands of years—which is its greatest tool against us. The men who benefit don't even have to try that hard anymore to get us to do what they want: We do it for them. As Monica Sjöö and Barbara Mor wrote:

> "Colonialism is a form of vampirism that empowers and bloats the self-image of the colonizing empire by draining the life energies of the colonized people; just enough blood is left to allow the colonial subject to perform a day's work for the objective empire. And these drained energies are not only of the present and future, but of the past, of memory itself: the continuity of identity of a people, and of each individual who is colonized.
>
> No one should recognize this process better than women; for the female sex has functioned as a colony of organized patriarchal power for several thousand years now. Our brains have been emptied out of all memory of our own cultural history, and the colonizing power systematically denies such a history ever existed. The colonizing power mocks our attempts to rediscover and celebrate our ancient matriarchies as realities. In the past women have had to accept this enforced female amnesia as "normal"; and many contemporary women continue to believe the female sex has existed always and ab aeterno as an auxiliary to the male-dominated world order. But we continue to dig in the ruins, seeking the energy of memory; believing that the reconstruction of women's ancient

---

[136] Lerner, Gerda. *The Creation of Patriarchy.* Oxford University Press; 1987.

history has a revolutionary potential equal to that of any political movement today."[137]

Fortunately, you don't have to re-create the wheel yourself. There are at least a hundred years of excellent feminist writings by our foremothers to devour and learn from.

We must begin to look at our own HerStory and demand men who do the same. We cannot put a band-aid over the original lie of rebranding God as male. Until we return to an understanding that woman creates life—and always had created ALL life, women will continue to be subordinated.

We are not the equals to men. We are the Creators of men. Males have been trying to suppress this fact for thousands of years. There are many recommended books listed at the back of this book to get you started, but there is also a lot of information available online. Learn about African history and Native American history. Everything they don't teach in school will have value to you and give you a broader perspective. I think the schools are doing a little better now—but I didn't learn any of this until college and then I ate it up.

If you are not following Max Dashu's *Suppressed Histories Archives*, you need to do so right now. Max has spent over 40 years uncovering what has been suppressed by men in power. I had the privilege of following Max on her NW Tour several years ago with my daughter. It was life-changing! There were many women in tears hearing their history for the first time—and I was thrilled that my 8-year-old daughter was getting an early start. We must begin to learn our HERstory earlier.

---

[137] Sjöö, Monica and Mor, Barbara. *The Great Cosmic Mother: Rediscovering the Religion of the Earth*. HarperOne; 2nd edition, 1987.

Read & Write as if your Life Depended on It

You may have already noted that I love to read. Reading has always been my refuge, but as I get older I realize it has also been my salvation. As Gerda Lerner wrote, "Perhaps the greatest challenge to thinking women is the challenge to move from the desire for safety and approval to the most 'unfeminine' quality of all—that of intellectual arrogance, the supreme hubris which asserts to itself the right to reorder the world. The Hubris of the god makers, the hubris of the male-system builders."[138]

I read a lot, so I am always looking for ways to save money. When I was a single mother, I did not have any extra money for anything, let alone books. Fortunately, the Portland library was amazing. I would often return with stacks of 10 or 15 books. I was able to order just about anything I wanted to read online and pick up the books as they became available.

The library in Bergen is not as good for the English books I would like to read, so I often utilize the free sample on Kindle before I decide to buy. You can read about 20% of most books for free. And, many authors give away books for free on Kindle occasionally. Follow the authors you like—and join my mailing list if you want to see such offers from me.

When you buy books, purchase them from the author herself instead of Amazon whenever possible, as they take most of the profits—or support your local bookstore. I know other women who enjoy Kindle and listening to audio books. There is a huge variety of (free) audio books on YouTube. Listening to audio books was the only way I could 'read' when my children were young.

---

[138] Lerner, Gerda. *The Creation of Patriarchy*. Oxford University Press; 1987.

Reading has become a lost art. Andrea Dworkin made a connection long ago that I am finally beginning to see.

> "I love books the way I love nature. I can imagine now that someday there will be no nature, at least not as we knew it together on Crete, no mysterious ocean, no luminous sky, no stark and unsettled mountains. I can imagine now that a time will come, that it is almost upon us, when no one will love books, that there will be no people who need them the way some of us need them now—like food and air, sunshine and warmth. It is no accident, I think, that books and nature (as we know it) may disappear simultaneously from human experience. There is no mind-body split."

There is something very subversive about taking time out to read a real book. There is also something about writing your own narrative that is hugely empowering. Mona Eltahawy wrote that, "The most subversive thing a woman can do is talk about her life as if it really matters."[139] Whether or not you want to publish what you write about your life is up to you. But just the act of talking and writing about our lives is empowering. Men have controlled the dominant narratives for too long. We must begin to find our own voices—and support other women and girls in doing so as well.

---

[139] Eltahawy, Mona. *Headscarves and Hymens: Why the Middle East Needs a Sexual Revolution*. Farrar, Straus and Giroux; 2016.

Healing Modalities

I want to bring up some healing work that has helped me. I realize that much of this may not be free—however it is also possible to trade or learn how to do some of this yourself. This comes back to the principal of investing in yourself. If you feel that you cannot afford something to facilitate your own healing, give careful thought as to how you might be able to restructure your budget, trade services or learn to do something yourself. It may take some creativity, but the reward will be worth it.

As Gabor Maté notes, "For those habituated to high levels of internal stress since childhood, it is the absence of stress that creates unease, evoking boredom and a sense of meaninglessness. Many people become addicted to their own stress hormones, adrenaline and cortisol, Hans Selye observed. To such persons, stress feels desirable, while the absence of it is something to be avoided.[140]" For this reason, I have used a lot of healing modalities to break some of these patterns in my own life.

Starting with free, I almost always have YouTube meditations playing while I work. My go-to is a video my sister sent me about 5 years ago with the promise that it would change my brainwave frequencies for the better when feeling anxious or stressed!— *Schumann Resonance 7.83hz Isochronic Tones, With Underwater Sounds and Whales.* I also listened to these types of meditations extensively after my surgery—all night long for many weeks in fact. If I feel tired, I go for *Whole Body Regeneration*. When I am worried, I listen to *LET GO of Fear, Overthinking and Worries*." If you search, you can find meditations for just about anything.

I also utilize essential oils now that I have more disposable income. Back to sharing, if you can afford to use these, consider

---

140 Maté, Gabor. *When the Body Says No: Understanding the Stress-Disease Connection.* Wiley; 2011.

buying an extra bottle or two to share with a woman who cannot —especially if they have young children. I have noted a big difference in our home since we have begun using them.

After my divorce, I could no longer afford to get massages or acupuncture. My Russian acupuncturist told me that the fire cupping she did was actually something that the grandmothers taught everyone in the village. So, with some help from her, YouTube, and a little trial and error—I learned how to cup myself. I do not recommend this to everyone. I was *desperate*. And I have burned myself, once fairly severely. But it was worth it to me. I got the care I needed for my back, and I now know how to do this to myself and my family safely.

My husband gives me a full body massage almost every night. So, this is something to consider if you have a partner. Prior to that, I gave myself a fully body massage every morning before my shower. I stopped doing this after we moved in together but started again recently because I feel so much better doing it.

Massage has numerous benefits—and for those of us who have stored a lot of trauma in our bodies, it can be invaluable. If you have children, you can also do what I did when I was a desperate single mom and have them walk (carefully) on your back. *Whatever works!*

I do not use any store-bought creams or oils on my body because most have chemicals in them I do not want to absorb. So, I have made my own oils for more than 16 years. This is also considerably less expensive.

When I was pregnant with my son, my once lush skin turned flaky and red. Nothing seemed to help. I finally began to make my own natural and organic oils because so many oils and lotions are filled with crap—and I did not want my son exposed to any of that. I like to know what I am putting into my body, just like I like knowing exactly what I am eating.

Most mornings I start my day with a self-massage before my shower. I usually start at my neck and work my way down my breasts, arms, stomach, back-side and legs. It only takes 5 minutes, but it is so good for your immune system, circulation and overall energy. Not to mention that my skin feels like "butter," as several people have told me...

Making the oil is easy. You can buy everything you need for about $30, and it will last you about 6 months. It will take about 10 minutes to mix everything and put it back into bottles. Trader Joe's has good deals on Vitamin E oil and coconut oil if you are in the United States. The other oils I buy at a natural food store. It is best to buy organic oils if possible.

Here is my recipe:

> 1 jar of coconut oil
> 1 bottle of vitamin E oil
> 1 bottle of avocado oil
> 1 bottle of almond or walnut oil
> a drop of essential oil (if you want some extra fragrance)

Soften the coconut oil and mix everything together. Put the oil back into the bottles or into pumping containers for easier application.

Chakra Balancing

All 7 chakras must be balanced to allow energy to flow throughout the body in an optimal way. Paola Suarez has a guest post on my blog about how to ground and energize your chakras.[141]

---

[141] Suarez, Paola. "Ground and Energize Your Chakras in 10 Minutes!"

A good basic book on this is *Chakra Balancing* by Anodea Judith, which is sold as a complete chakra balancing set, including CDs. There are probably hundreds of free meditations available on YouTube though, so take some time to check them out and see what works best for you.

If you have trauma in your background, check out *Truth Heals* by Deborah King. I have been working on balancing my chakras for many years, but this is the first book I have seen that really delves into the trauma aspect of it. Many thanks to my dear friend Susan Morgaine who sent it to me recently.

Reiki

The International Center for Reiki Training describes Reiki as "a Japanese technique for stress reduction and relaxation that also promotes healing. It is administered by 'laying on hands' and is based on the idea that an unseen 'life force energy' flows through us and is what causes us to be alive. If one's 'life force energy' is low, then we are more likely to get sick or feel stress, and if it is high, we are more capable of being happy and healthy."[142]

It is important to find a good practitioner. I met with someone in Portland and just felt *meh* afterwards. I didn't look into doing Reiki again until after my children's father died and I was desperate.

We all did sessions to clear out toxicity at this time, and I did additional work on clearing blockages created by sexual abuse. This is not free obviously—but can be well worth the money if you can afford it—or find someone to trade services with.

---

[142] "What is Reiki?" The International Center for Reiki Training. Copyright 2019.

Tapping

If you struggle with invasive thoughts or have trauma, tapping is something to look into. This is beyond the scope of this book, but you can access a lot of tapping meditations online. Dr. Mercola has several links available on his website—or check out Nick or Jessica Ortner, both of whom have best-selling books on the subject and loads of information available for free online.

Acupuncture

Acupuncture has saved my sanity and restored my health many a time. It is not cheap—although I know some cities have clinics that are more communal and you can get a treatment that is relatively inexpensive. Learning acupressure points can also be also be enormously helpful, especially if you suffer from headaches or menstrual cramps.

When Things Feel Irreparably Shitty

There are some things in your life that are absolutely horrible in Capitalist Patriarchy. For example, the six months I spent in "Family Court" were the worst and most stressful months of my entire life.

If you must be involved in a system like this—that is entirely drenched in male preference—there is little you can do to make it great while you are stuck there.[143]

You just have to get through it the best you can. This becomes easier when you work on healing your life and come at it from a grounded and centered place. Oriah Mountain Dreamer wrote:

> "When we know our wholeness, when we are consciously aware of both ego and essence, we feel the pain of loss in our lives not as crippling devastation that makes us want to give up on life itself, but as human sadness that we know will change with time as all feelings do...
>
> Awareness of the essence of what we are does not take us away from our feelings, but it can give us a perspective that makes it easier to be with these feelings without identifying exclusively with, suffering painfully over or acting upon them."[144]

---

[143] My anthology on single mothers and the upcoming book on financial abuse are both available as a free PDF to any woman who cannot afford them. As more of us heal, we have the ability to help our sisters through these difficulties and navigate out of the pitfalls that entrap us. One of the reasons books are important to me is that I feel they can help more women get through deplorable situations.

[144] Mountain Dreamer, Oriah. *The Call: Discovering Why You Are Here.* HarperOne; 2006.

When you go through difficult periods, make sure you have a community of friends and family around you to provide support. This is the time to lean on people, in whatever capacity they can provide relief or help.

It is also the time to see who your real friends—and the family you chose for yourself—really are. Some people you would expect to help you *won't,* but others will rise to the occasion and be there for you in ways you never imagined. I can't begin to count how many people left me when I lost everything. I rebuilt. Mostly from scratch. And, my life is richer for it.

When you feel hopeless—take a bath or a walk or a nap. Call a friend. Put on your favorite song. Read a book. Do anything that brings back the hope and the joy. If you need a day to wallow, take it. Nothing lasts forever—good or bad.

Join the Revolution!

Matriarchal researcher Heide Göttner-Abendroth recently demanded that, "Half of the world's assets should be used to finance women's projects," noting that women own only one percent of world wealth. She went on to say that, "Women make two-thirds of the working hours worldwide, but receive only one-tenth of the world's income."[145]

The truth is that we must soon move beyond individual healing and personal empowerment to **overthrow this entire system!** Imagine the world we could live in if war and poverty ceased to exist. Imagine no rape or sexual abuse.

Bad things will always happen to women and children under patriarchy: That is how it was designed. Patriarchy abuses, rapes, bankrupts, addicts and destroys women. We must fight it systematically and individually. If you want to confront patriarchy in your life, refuse to bow down anymore—and better yet, enjoy your life to the fullest extent possible.

Sometimes life isn't fair. Some people die young or spend a lifetime in poverty—while others seem to always come out on top. It is pretty much the luck of the draw, so you must make the most of whatever you get. The East understands what the West does not yet: Life is meant to be shared and celebrated.

We all have the potential for great joy in our lives. I remember thinking for at least a decade that I was doomed to be unhappy and decided I would just live with it. BULLSHIT. I worked on myself for years, but it wasn't until my Reiki practitioner looked into my soul and told me, "You have the potential for great joy—your inner being is actually quite joyful"—that I finally believed (and

---

[145] Michael Caspar, Von. "Werben für neues Matriarchat." *Goettinger Tageblatt,* 05.10.2018. Google Translate was used to translate this article from the original German into English.

then acted) differently. Remember Patricia Lynn Reilly's words, which have remained my mantra the last 8 years.

> "Daughter of Woman, your healing task is not to become a new, improved or changed person. Rather, it is to reclaim your natural and essential self in all its fullness. In the very beginning, you remembered yourself. You came into the world with feelings of omnipotence, not inferiority."[146]

All of us are a work in progress. But don't let the work get in the way of living. Live the life you have now—to the fullest. As Nayyirah Waheed admonished, "do not choose the lesser life. do you hear me. *do you hear me*. choose the life that is. yours. the life that is seducing your lungs. that is dripping down your chin."[147]

You are stronger than you ever realized—and the spirits of your ancestors and our feminist foremothers are always with you.

We must not settle any longer for the man-made mess that was created with patriarchy. Vanessa Olorenshaw wrote:

> "As feminists, we must start to demand that our political and economic systems live up to our dreams, for ourselves and our children. The fact that we don't is a telling demonstration of that old chestnut: we are silenced out of fear or shame, of not wanting to want too much, not wanting to demand or expect, lest we overstep our mark. Thing is, if we don't speak up, if we don't demand the political system reflect rather than dictate, nothing is going to improve."[148]

---

[146] Reilly, Patricia Lynn. *Be Full of Yourself!: The Journey from Self-Criticism to Self-Celebration.* Open Window Creations; 1998.

[147] Waheed, Nayyirah. n*ejma.* Createspace; 2014.

[148] Orenshaw, Vanessa. *Liberating Motherhood: Birthing the Purplestockings Movement.* Womancraft Publishing; 2016.

I believe women need more inner work and consciousness raising versus the intellectual aspects of feminism. Feminist theory is useless unless it makes women's everyday lives not only "better" but *blissful*. Beatrix Campbell ended her manifesto with, "Imagine men without violence. Imagine sex without violence. Imagine that men stop stealing our stuff—our time, our money and our bodies; imagine societies that share the costs of care, that share the costs of everything; that make cities fit for children; that renew rather than wreck and waste. This is women's liberation. It is do-able, reasonable and revolutionary."[149]

We must begin to reclaim the lives we thirst for—and stop reinforcing the tyranny we were dictated. The structure we uphold is the one that will prevail. Gerda Lerna wrote that, "The system of patriarchy is a historic construct; it has a beginning; it will have an end. Its time seems to have nearly run its course—it no longer serves the needs of men or women and in its inextricable linkage to militarism, hierarchy, and racism it threatens the very existence of life on earth."[150]

There is no greater reward than living a great life despite a system that intends to obliterate you. As Alice Walker wrote, "Resistance is the secret of joy."[151]

Together, we can do this. I know we can.

---

[149] Campbell, Beatrix End of Equality: *The Only Way Is Women's Liberation*. Seagull Books; 2014.
[150] Lerner, Gerda. *The Creation of Patriarchy*. Oxford University Press; 1987.
[151] Walker, Alice. *Possessing the Secret of Joy*. The New Press; 2008.

"You have escaped the cage.
Your wings are stretched out.
Now fly."

-Rumi

Imagine a Woman...

Until we imagine something, it remains an impossibility. Once imagined, it becomes our experience.

Imagine a woman who loves herself. A woman who gazes with loving kindness upon her past and present, body and needs, ideas and emotions. Whose capacity to love others deepens as she extends loving kindness to herself.

Imagine a woman who accepts herself. A woman who turns a merciful eye toward her own secrets, successes, and shortcomings. Whose capacity to live non-judgmentally deepens as she is merciful toward herself.

Imagine a woman who participates in her own life with interest and attention. A woman who turns inward to listen, remember, and replenish. Whose capacity to be available deepens as she is available to herself.

Imagine a woman who remains faithful to herself through the seasons of life. A woman who preserves allegiance to herself even when opposed. Whose capacity to sustain interest in others deepens as she is loyal to herself.

Imagine a woman who bites into her own life and the fullness of its possibility. A woman who has opened to the depths of goodness within her. Who affirms the original goodness of her children until the stories of old hold no sway in their hearts.

Imagine a community of women who rock the world by giving birth to images of inclusion, poems of truth, rituals of healing, experiences of transformation, relationships of equality, strategies of peace, institutions of justice, and households of compassion for the sake of our children's future.

Imagine a world where the question, "What's wrong with me" has been exorcised from the bodies and lives of our daughters. A world where they cultivate their amazing capacities as children of life. Where they travel a less turbulent path than we did toward self-love, self-acceptance, and self-trust.

Imagine yourself as this woman. And together let us imagine such a community and world into being for the sake of our daughters and sons, and our beloved planet.

-Patricia Lynn Reilly, Imagine a Woman III
Copyright, 2014

Suggested Reading

A Deeper Wisdom: The 12 Steps from a Woman's Perspective – Patricia Lynn Reilly

A God Who Looks Like Me – Patricia Lynn Reilly

A Happier Hour – Rebecca Weller

A Mind of Your Own: The Truth About Depression and How Women Can Heal Their Bodies to Reclaim Their Lives – Kelly Brogan M.D.

Ain't I a Woman: Black Women and Feminism – bell hooks

All About Love: New Visions – bell hooks

Aphrodite's Magic: Celebrate and Heal Your Sexuality – Jane Meredith

Be Full of Yourself: The Journey from Self-Criticism to Self-Celebration – Patricia Lynn Reilly

Beyond God the Father: Toward a Philosophy of Women's Liberation – Mary Daly

Blood, Bread, and Roses: How Menstruation Created the World – Judy Grahn

Braiding Sweetgrass: Indigenous Wisdom, Scientific Knowledge and the Teachings of Plants – Robin Wall Kimmerer

Breaking Down the Wall of Silence: The Liberating Experience of Facing Painful Truth – Alice Miller

Buffalo Woman Comes Singing – Brooke Medicine Eagle

Burning Woman – Lucy Pearce

Caliban and the Witch: Women, the Body and Primitive Accumulation – Silvia Federici

Chakra Balancing – Anodea Judith

Communion: The Female Search for Love – bell hooks

Cunt: a declaration of independence – Inga Muscio

Cyborgs Versus the Earth Goddess: Men's Domestication of Women and Animals and Female Resistance – Moses Seenarine

Dodging Energy Vampires: An Empath's Guide to Evading Relationships That Drain You and Restoring Your Health – Christiane Northrup M.D.

Eating in the Light of the Moon: How Women Can Transform Their Relationship with Food Through Myths, Metaphors, and Storytelling – Anita A. Johnson PhD.

Effortless Healing: 9 Simple Ways to Sidestep Illness, Shed Excess Weight, and Help Your Body Fix Itself – Dr Joseph Mercola

Emerging from Broken; the Beginning of Hope for Emotional Healing – Darlene Ouimet

End of Equality: The Only Way Is Women's Liberation – Beatrix Campbell

Feminist Spirituality under Capitalism: Witches, Fairies, and Nomads – Kathleen Skott-Myhre

Feminist Theory: From Margin to Center – bell hooks

Foremothers of Women's Spirituality – Edited by Vicki Noble and Miriam Robbins Dexter

For-giving: A Feminist Criticism of Exchange – Genevieve Vaughan

Goddesses Never Age: The Secret Prescription for Radiance, Vitality, and Well-Being – Christiane Northrup M.D.

Going Out of Our Minds: The Metaphysics of Liberation – Sonia Johnson

Gyn/Ecology: The Metaethics of Radical Feminism – Mary Daly

Healing Magic: A Green Witch Guidebook to Conscious Living – Robin Rose Bennett

Heartbreak – Andrea Dworkin

Her Best Kept Secret: Why Women Drink—And How They Can Regain Control – Gabrielle Glaser

In Search of Our Mothers' Gardens: Womanist Prose – Alice Walker

I Promise Myself: Making a Commitment to Yourself and Your Dreams – Patricia Lynn Reilly

Imagine a Woman in Love with Herself: Embracing Your Wisdom and Wholeness – Patricia Lynn Reilly

In Her Image – Kathie Carlson

Intercourse – Andrea Dworkin

It's a Shareable Life: A Practical Guide on Sharing – Gabriel Stempinski, Alexandra Liss and Chelsea Rustrum

It's Not Your Money – Tosha Silver

Jailbreak: The Secret Liberation System for High-Achieving Women / Identifying and Healing Patriarchy Stress Disorder – Dr. Valerie Rein

Liberating Motherhood: Birthing the Purplestockings Movement – Vanessa Olorenshaw

Light in the Dark/Luz en lo Oscuro: Rewriting Identity, Spirituality, Reality – Gloria E. Anzaldúa

Liver Rescue – Anthony William

Love Warrior: A Memoir – Glennon Doyle

Loving to Survive: Sexual Terror, Men's Violence & Women's Lives – Dee R. Graham

Madness & Oppression: Paths to Personal Transformation and Collective Liberation – The Icarus Project

Make Your Creative Dreams Real: A Plan for Procrastinators, Perfectionists, Busy People, and People Who Would Really Rather Sleep – Sark

Malcolm X: The Last Speeches – Malcolm X

Many Roads One Journey: Moving Beyond the 12 Steps – Charlotte Davis Kasl

Matri: Letters from the Mother – Zoe Ann Nicholson

Medicine Woman – Lucy Pearce

Matriarchal Societies: Studies on Indigenous Cultures Across the Globe – Heide Göttner-Abendroth

Mouth Matters; How Your Mouth Ages Your Body and What YOU Can Do About It – Carol Vander Stoep

My Abundant Universe: Prosperity and the Path of Least Resistance – Arna Baartz

New Love: a reprogramming toolbox for undoing the knots – Trista Hendren and Arna Baartz

New Menopausal Years: Alternative Approaches for Women 30-90 – Susun S. Weed

Of Woman Born: Motherhood as Experience and Institution – Adrienne Rich

Overcoming Underearning™: A Simple Guide to a Richer Life – Barbara Stanny

PaGaian Cosmology: Re-inventing Earth-based Goddess Religion – Glenys Livingstone

Pornland: How Porn Has Hijacked Our Sexuality – Gail Dines

Pornography: Men Possessing Women – Andrea Dworkin

Prince Charming Isn't Coming: How Women Get Smart About Money – Barbara Stanny

QUINTESSENCE: Realizing the Archaic Future A Radical Elemental Feminist Manifesto – Mary Daly

Rage Becomes Her: The Power of Women's Anger – Soraya Chemaly

Rebirth of the Goddess: Finding Meaning in Feminist Spirituality – Carol P. Christ

Recovering the Sacred: The Power of Naming and Claiming – Winona LaDuke

Revolution at Point Zero: Housework, Reproduction, and Feminist Struggle – Silvia Federici

Secret Bad Girl: A Sexual Trauma Memoir and Resolution Guide – Rachael Maddox

She Rises: Why Goddess Feminism, Activism or Spirituality? – Edited by Dr. Helen Hwang and Dr. Kaalii Cargill

She Who Changes: Re-imagining the Divine in the World – Carol P. Christ

Sister Outsider – Audre Lorde

Sisterhood is Forever – Robin Morgan

Sisterhood is Global – Robin Morgan

Spark Joy: An Illustrated Master Class on the Art of Organizing and Tidying Up – Marie Kondō

Splendor: The Nazarite Method to Re(growing) Long, Strong, Healthy, Holy Hair – Sara Eisenman

Succulent Wild Woman: Dancing with Your Wonder-Full Self – Sark

Sula – Toni Morrison

Sweetening the Pill: or How We Got Hooked on Hormonal Birth Control – Holly Grigg-Spall

The Adrenal Thyroid Revolution: A Proven 4-Week Program to Rescue Your Metabolism, Hormones, Mind & Mood – Aviva Romm, M.D.

The Alcohol Experiment: A 30-day, Alcohol-Free Challenge to Interrupt Your Habits and Help You Take Control – Annie Grace

The Art of Extreme Self-Care – Cheryl Richardson

The Art of Money: A Life-Changing Guide to Financial Happiness – Bari Tessler

The Art of Sexual Ecstasy – Margo Anand

The Body Keeps the Score: Brain, Mind, and Body in the Healing of Trauma – Bessel van der Kolk MD

The Bones, The Breaking, The Balm: A Colored Girl's Hymnal – Dominique Christina

The Chalice and The Blade – Riane Eisler

The Church and the Second Sex – Mary Daly

The Civilization of the Goddess – Marija Gimbutas

The Color Purple – Alice Walker

The Courage to Heal: A Guide for Women Survivors of Child Sexual Abuse – Ellen Bass and Laura Davis

The Creation of Feminist Consciousness – Gerda Lerner

The Creation of Patriarchy – Gerda Lerner

The Dance of the Dissident Daughter – Sue Monk Kidd

The Eight Human Talents: Restore the Balance and Serenity within You with Kundalini Yoga Paperback – Gurmukh and Cathryn Michon

The Encyclopedia of Women's Myths and Secrets – Barbara G. Walker

The Great Cosmic Mother – Monica Sjöö & Barbara Mor

The Highly Sensitive Person: How to Thrive When the World Overwhelms You – Elaine Aron PhD

The Holy Book of Women's Mysteries – Zsuzsanna Budapest

The Life-Changing Magic of Tidying Up: The Japanese Art of Decluttering and Organizing – Marie Kondō

The Mago Way: Re-discovering Mago, the Great Goddess from East Asia – Helen Hye-Sook Hwang, Ph.D.

The Mastery of Love – Don Miguel Ruiz

The Non-Tinfoil Guide to EMFs: How to Fix Our Stupid Use of Technology – Nicolas Pineault

The Obsidian Mirror – Louise M. Wisechild

The Real Wealth of Nations – Riane Eisler

The Red Tent – Anita Diamant

The Sacred Hoop: Recovering the Feminine in American Indian – Paula Gunn Allen

The Soul of Money: Transforming Your Relationship with Money and Life – Lynne Twist

The Spiral Dance: A Rebirth of the Ancient Religion of the Goddess – Starhawk

The Tapping Solution to Create Lasting Change: A Guide to Get Unstuck and Find Your Flow – Jessica Ortner

The Verbally Abusive Relationship: How to recognize it and how to respond – Patricia Evans

The Wisdom of Menopause: Creating Physical and Emotional Health During the Change – Christiane Northrup M.D.

This Bridge Called My Back – Gloria Anzaldua and Cherríe Moraga

This Naked Mind: Control Alcohol, Find Freedom, Discover Happiness & Change Your Life – Annie Grace

This is Woman's Work: Calling Forth Your Inner Council of Wise, Brave, Crazy, Rebellious, Loving, Luminous Selves – Dominique Christina

Trauma and Recovery: The Aftermath of Violence–From Domestic Abuse to Political Terror – Judith Herman

Truth Heals: What You Hide Can Hurt You – Deborah King

Victory Over Verbal Abuse: A Healing Guide to Renewing Your Spirit and Reclaiming Your Life – Patricia Evans

Wages for Housework – Silvia Federici

When the Body Says No: Understanding the Stress-Disease Connection – Gabor Maté

When God Was a Woman – Merlin Stone

When Women Were Birds: Fifty-four Variations on Voice – Terry Tempest Williams

Why Does He Do That? Inside the Minds of Angry and Controlling Men – Lundy Bancroft

Why Women Have Better Sex Under Socialism: And Other Arguments for Economic Independence – Kristen R. Ghodsee

Wild Mercy: Living the Fierce and Tender Wisdom of the Women Mystics – Marabai Starr

Wildfire: Igniting the She/Volution – Sonia Johnson

Witches and Pagans: Women in European Folk Religion – Max Dashu

Witches, Witch-Hunting, and Women – Silvia Federici

WOLFPACK: How to Come Together, Unleash Our Power, and Change the Game – Abby Wambach

Woman Hating – Andrea Dworkin

Woman and Nature: The Roaring Inside Her – Susan Griffin

Woman's Inhumanity to Women – Phyllis Chesler

Women and the Gift Economy: A Radically Different Worldview is Possible – Genevieve Vaughan

Women, Sex, and Addiction: A Search for Love and Power – Charlotte Davis Kasl

Women's Bodies, Women's Wisdom: Creating Physical and Emotional Health and Healing – Christiane Northrup M.D.

Women's Rites, Women's Mysteries – Ruth Barrett

Women's Spirituality: Power and Grace – Mary Faulker

Writing Alone Together: Journalling in a Circle of Women for Creativity, Compassion and Connection – Ahava Shira PhD, Wendy Judith Cutler MA and Lynda Monk MSW

You Can Heal Your Life – Louise Hay

Acknowledgments

My friend Monica recently asked me why I had decided to drastically change and heal my life many years ago. The answer is simple—my children.

When I became pregnant with my son, **Joey**, I knew I had to learn how to do things different for his sake.

My daughter, **Helani**, taught me that I must continue to fight for women and girls everywhere so that her life would not be hampered the way mine was under patriarchy.

I wish to thank my beloved husband **Anders** for his endless support, love and patience as I have journeyed through my healing process and recovery.

I wish to thank my mother, **Pat**, for her never-ending support of me—and for editing this book, and all my others.

I would like to acknowledge my closest sister-friends, **Tamara** and **Susan**—who I chat with constantly every single day. You are my anchors. And, of course, my dear Sis **Alyscia Cunningham**—to whom my words can never fully convey my admiration and appreciation.

Special thanks to **Arna Baartz** for the gorgeous cover art, the original of which is framed (and cherished) in my bedroom.

All my love to **Goddess**, who speaks to me through my innermost being and girl child—as well as my ancestors, particularly my grandmothers, **Marge** and **JoAnne.**

About the Author

Trista Hendren is the creator of The Girl God series
and a Certified Coach with Imagine a Woman International.
Read more about her projects at www.thegirlgod.com

Made in United States
Troutdale, OR
07/09/2023

11084869R00105